Joann,

Hope you enjoy. It's full of stories of God's & love for us. It's great getting to meet all of our new neighbors here at West End Flats.

In Christ

[signature]

610-328-1553
5-12-19
Apt #04

# I AM, THEREFORE I KNOW

*What Brings Peace, Joy, Happiness and Hope?*

R. W. MILLS

authorHOUSE®

*AuthorHouse*™
*1663 Liberty Drive*
*Bloomington, IN 47403*
*www.authorhouse.com*
*Phone: 1 (800) 839-8640*

© 2017 R. W. Mills. All rights reserved.

No part of this book may be reproduced, stored in a retrieval system, or transmitted by any means without the written permission of the author.

Published by AuthorHouse  04/28/2017

ISBN: 978-1-5246-8999-5 (sc)
ISBN: 978-1-5246-9000-7 (hc)
ISBN: 978-1-5246-8998-8 (e)

Library of Congress Control Number: 2017906626

Print information available on the last page.

Any people depicted in stock imagery provided by Thinkstock are models, and such images are being used for illustrative purposes only.
Certain stock imagery © Thinkstock.

This book is printed on acid-free paper.

Because of the dynamic nature of the Internet, any web addresses or links contained in this book may have changed since publication and may no longer be valid. The views expressed in this work are solely those of the author and do not necessarily reflect the views of the publisher, and the publisher hereby disclaims any responsibility for them.

The Holy Bible, Berean Study Bible, BSB
Copyright ©2016 by Bible Hub
Used by Permission. All Rights Reserved Worldwide.

Scripture quotations marked NIV are taken from the Holy Bible, New International Version®. NIV®. Copyright © 1973, 1978, 1984 by International Bible Society. Used by permission of Zondervan. All rights reserved. [Biblica]

# Contents

Introduction .................................................................... vii

| Chapter 1 | I AM ................................................................ 1 |
| Chapter 2 | PREDESTINED ............................................. 13 |
| Chapter 3 | FREE WILL ................................................... 17 |
| Chapter 4 | WHOSOEVER ............................................... 31 |
| Chapter 5 | UNDERSTAND ............................................. 40 |
| Chapter 6 | TRANSFORMATION .................................... 47 |
| Chapter 7 | DISCIPLESHIP .............................................. 54 |
| Chapter 8 | DIFFERENCES .............................................. 72 |
| Chapter 9 | MORE THAN A FAN ................................... 108 |
| Chapter 10 | CONCLUSION ............................................ 119 |

Appendix ..................................................................... 125

# INTRODUCTION

**W**hat *brings peace, joy, happiness and hope?* I can only share what has provided these to me. The Bible - yes, the Holy Scriptures. It is a book that contains more insight about human behavior and has in it the greatest words ever written. This love story reveals to us what God wants us to know about Him, His creation, and His plan for each of our lives.

- In <u>Acts 17:26-28</u>, it states that God decides where and when we would live: "From one man he made every nation of men, that they should inhabit the whole earth; ***and he determined the times set for them and the exact places where they should live.*** God did this so that ***they would seek him and <u>perhaps</u> reach out for him and find him,*** though ***he is not far*** from any one of us. 'For in him we live and move and have our being.' As some of your own poets have said, 'We are his offspring.'"[1]

God determines when and where we shall live. God does not stop there. God is personally involved in the lives of each and every human being from the beginning of time. He does it for one purpose: so each would seek Him and **PERHAPS** reach out and find Him. He is not far from any of us. We are His offspring, His children.

God reveals to us, in Romans, that He has placed knowledge of Himself in each of us. We know He is and should seek Him. Later in Romans He reveals that He has written His laws on our hearts and has given us a conscience. God has revealed in His Word that He knew each of us before the foundations of the world. Psalms 139 states that He perceives

---

[1] All verses are New International Version (NIV) unless noted.

our thoughts, and before a word is said, He knows it. Listen to what King David says:

- Psalm 139:1-8, 13-16:"You have searched me, LORD, and you **know me**. You know when I sit and when I rise; you perceive my thoughts from afar. You discern my going out and my lying down; you are familiar with all my ways. **Before a word is on my tongue you, LORD, *know* it completely.** You hem me in behind and before, and you lay your hand upon me. Such knowledge is too wonderful for me, too lofty for me to attain. Where can I go from your Spirit? Where can I flee from your presence? If I go up to the heavens, you are there; if I make my bed in the depths, you are there… For you created my inmost being; you knit me together in my mother's womb. I praise you because I am fearfully and wonderfully made; your works are wonderful, I know that full well. My frame was not hidden from you when I was made in the secret place, when I was woven together in the depths of the earth. Your eyes saw my unformed body; *all the days ordained for me were written in your book before one of them came to be.*"

This means that before God created the heavens and earth He knew us. He had a plan and He chose to reveal His progressive revelation to His offspring over time. As the title of this book states: I AM, Therefore I Know. It means that **He knows all** about everything, even to the intimate level of a single person's thoughts. His Word states not a single hair falls without His knowledge. In Hebrews, the word "yada" means much more than knowledge. It is about intimacy. God wants that in our relationship with Him. Really? I could not believe that God honestly desired an intimate relationship with someone like me.

I will do my best to share how God and His amazing revelation, voiced in the Holy Scriptures, helped me understand the person of God, so that I could receive His peace, His joy, His Happiness and now have a Hope that fuels my love for Him, which has changed how I see the world.

## Chapter 1

# I AM

## WHO IS GOD AS REVEALED BY GOD?

Who and what is God? The definition found in the Westminster Catechism: "God is Spirit, infinite, eternal, and unchangeable in His being, wisdom, power, holiness, justice, goodness and truth." The scriptural definition can be developed from a study of the names of God.

→ **Elohim** is the Creator-God; translated "God."
→ **Jehovah** is the covenant God; which means He who was, is, and is to come; in other words the Eternal One. He reveals himself as follows:
  - **Jehovah-Rapha**, "the Lord that healeth."
  - **Jehovah-Nissi**, "the Lord our Banner."
  - **Jehovah-Shalom**, "the Lord our Peace."
  - **Jehovah-Ra'ah**, "the Lord my Shepherd."
  - **Jehovah-Tsidkenu**, "the Lord our Righteous."
  - **Jehovah-Jireh**, "the Lord who provides."
  - **Jehovah-Shammah**, "the Lord is there."
→ **Adonai** means literally "Lord" or "Master" and conveys the idea of rulership and dominion.
→ **Father** is employed in both the Old and New Testaments. However, the word Abba (Daddy), found in Galatians 4:6, indicates a much more personal level of relationship.
  - Galatians 4:6: "Because you are his sons, God sent the Spirit of his Son into our hearts, the Spirit who calls out, 'Abba, Father.'"

**The Attributes of God as revealed in Scripture:**
As God is infinite in His being, it is impossible for any creature to know Him exactly as He is. Yet, He has graciously willed to reveal Himself to us. The names of God express His whole being, while His attributes indicate various aspects of His character.

- → **God is Spirit.** He thinks, feels, speaks, and can therefore have direct communication with His creatures made in His image.
- → **God is Infinite.** That is, not subject to human limitations.
- → **God is One.** A perfect unity with three Divine Persons united in eternal and essential unity.
- → **God is Omnipotent.** This signifies two things: first, His freedom and power to do all that is consistent with His nature; second, His control and sovereignty over all that is or can be done.
- → **God is Omnipresent.** That is, unlimited by space. While God is everywhere, He does not dwell everywhere. He only enters into a personal relationship based on a personal invitation.
- → **God is Wise.** He has the power to supply His knowledge so that the best possible purposes are realized by the best possible means. God always does the right thing, in the right way, and at the right time.
- → **God is Sovereign.** That is, He has an absolute right to govern and dispose of His creatures as He pleases. Therefore, it is both foolish and wicked to criticize His ways.
- → **God is Holy.** The holiness of God means His absolute moral purity. He can neither sin nor tolerate sin.
- → **God is Love.** Love is the attribute by reason of which He desires a personal relationship with those who bear His image (His Word tells us that we are all made in His image). His love towards us is limitless/endless and desires all to come to Him.
- → **God is Good.** The goodness of God is that attribute by reason of which He imparts life and other blessings to His creatures.

The God of the Bible is a God on whom we can depend. He is unique, eternal, holy, powerful, majestic, compassionate, gracious, faithful, true, unchangeable and is actively present with His people. He is not a God who is arbitrary or capricious. His attributes ensure His expression towards us. He declares He is the "I AM" and worthy of our trust. He is master of all events, forces, and outcomes since He is totally sovereign. He has decided how history will play out. He is the one who can raise up one nation and bring destruction upon another. All is subject to his will and plans. He has created the universe that we are a part of, and our existence is dependent on him, even if we do not acknowledge him. Listen to the following verse:

- Romans 1:18-20: "The wrath of God is being revealed from heaven against all the godlessness and wickedness of people, who suppress the truth by their wickedness, since what may be known about God is plain to them, because God has made it plain to them. For since the creation of the world God's invisible qualities - **His eternal power and divine nature - have been clearly seen**, being understood from what has been made, *so that people are without excuse.*"

God has placed knowledge of Him in us. We see His invisible qualities, His power and divine nature. Why? So we would seek Him and we would be without excuse. God's wrath for disobedience of his laws, godlessness, wickedness, etc. has been built into the very structure of His universe. It is not capricious, impulsive, or an arbitrary outburst of anger. No, it is a settled determined response of a holy God. What God has shared to his offspring and children in His Holy Word is found in:

- Galatians 6:7: "Do not be deceived: God cannot be mocked. A man reaps what he sows."

Many people refer to this as karma. God could have created a completely different universe without free will, eternal laws designed to punish those who break them. If God is the Alpha and Omega, He is the Creator of all."

- Isaiah 45:7: "I form the light, and create darkness: I make peace, and create evil: I the Lord do all these things."

Since God is the Creator of all and evil exists, then God created evil. When God decided to make man in His image with free will, then the possibility of disobedience, sin, and evil was available. It was the same when God created light; darkness also was created.

- <u>Genesis 2:15-16:</u> "And the LORD God commanded them, 'You are free to eat from any tree in the garden; but you must not eat from the ***tree of the knowledge of good and evil***, for when you eat of it you will surely die.'"

This verse is the acknowledgement that evil exists. Anyone who lives long enough will encounter it and any review of human history can quickly provide enough examples of the working of evil.

I AM, Therefore I know. God's word tells us that before time as we know it began, there was only God in three distinct persons. God the Father, Christ His son and the Holy Spirit. All three are involved in creation. This means that when God decided what kind of universe there would be, He knew the ultimate cost. He knew there would be disobedience, sin, evil and death. He knew that His only Son would be sacrificed and die on the cross! The role of the Holy Spirit would dramatically change. Namely, the Holy Spirit's chief purpose now is to draw humans back to their loving Father through His gift of love to us – Jesus! As a parent, God knew that by giving us free will He would not be able to save all. Many would reject His love and His free gift of salvation.

People with hyperthymesia can remember almost everything that happened to them during their lives. They can remember things that happened to them in the crib, and can often recall in great detail every single event they've experienced, no matter how minor. They can remember that in March 2003 the U.S. invaded Iraq and it was a Wednesday. They can remember what they had for breakfast, lunch and dinner that day, too, and what they wore. For the parents of these children, it is a nightmare. Why? Because every misspoken word, every hurt that a parent inflicted, is remembered in detail forever. As I thought about this, I became overwhelmed with grief by the burden that God accepted with his creation of humankind: to know everything about each individual who turned away, to know you did everything in your power to save him or her, and then to remember every detail of your lost child perfectly and forever. The Holy Spirit showed me that only omnipotence can bear the burden of omniscience. ***God's shoulders were more than sufficient to carry the weight of infinite knowledge without losing joy.*** His Word tells us His love and mercy endure forever.

*I Am, Therefore I Know*

Our loving God – according to Acts 17:26 – selects our date of birth, our family and where we live. **Here is how God chose for me:** I was born a little over five pounds due to the fact that my mother was an alcoholic and a chain smoker (she died later in life of esophageal cancer). My father was an abusive alcoholic who had mental and emotional issues as a result of serving in the marines during WWII. His idea of communication involved physical beatings. I was one of four boys who was not to receive any real moral and religious training. My Dad's view of God was that whoever put the food on the table was your God. We had no parental training, let alone loving support or encouragement. This led me to becoming a hardened individual who trusted no one. I did not believe there was a God and lived like it.

I quickly learned to do whatever was necessary to survive. I started stealing from whatever resource I could find – stores, cars, trains, you name it. I remember my older brother taking me to steal my first bike. We rode for about two miles to a shopping center where people actually left their bikes unlocked. I still remember the rush I got from doing it. We then started stealing them so we could repaint them and sell them for cash. My father didn't know it, but I learned this philosophy from him, whose motto was to do unto others before they did it to you.

Our street had multiple drug operations, including my younger brother's drug business with many of my cousins who were from the next state over. The Warlocks and Pagans both would move in about two blocks from our home. Everything in our home was purchased from the underground economy. My Dad's car was a stolen car that was retitled and made legitimate by folks in the state transportation department who had their hands out. Everything from food, furniture, appliances, electronics, etc. was purchased illegally. I observed that, if you wanted something, it was available for much less on the underground economy. My Dad ran an illegal gambling operation, along with a bootleg alcohol business. I still remember my brother being arrested by the police for underage drinking and the police asking my Dad if he knew where the bootleg alcohol came from. He answered them with a confident "NO" without even flinching. Our home was visited many times by the local police, state police, and even the FBI stopped by a few times.

When I was ten I came home to find my older half-brother was no longer living at home. I was told that my older brother quit school, while he was in ninth grade, and went to live with our cousins in the next state. Later, I found out the truth. My brother was kicked out by my father. What do you think happened when I turned sixteen? I, too, was kicked out and started living anywhere I could. I was homeless for a short period of time. My mom already lost one son and threatened to shoot my father if I was not allowed back. My father took this seriously, since she had previously unloaded her 25 automatic clip at him. It was a good thing she was not a good shot. However, their bedroom wall did not fare as well!

All my friends were going nowhere. My best friend was into huffing. I remember him asking me why I would not huff, or do drugs like the rest of them. I told him that I hated my life which included my father, my home, my street, my poverty, basically everything. I said my only way out was to use every ounce of my brain, so I could not risk destroying it.

That brings me to school. School was a place where I wanted no one to know about my home situation. From the day I got my working papers in high school, I worked as a bus boy anywhere from twenty-four to thirty-two hours per week. Every Friday night I would take a trolley, then a bus, so I could work from 5:00 pm to 5:00 am after going to school that day. I would go get some sleep so I could return and do that same twelve hour shift again on Saturday night. Sunday was just four or eight hours depending on school or sports.

I still remember dozing in class when my ninth grade math teacher hit me in the chest with an eraser from his desk, which was over twenty-five feet away. Impressive, I thought. He then gave me the desk closest to him, but only after he called me a loser in front of the whole class. The midterm was coming up and I had a solid F so far. My verbal response was that he could not make a test on which I could not get an A, if I wanted. His response was a repeated "Loser"! I got A's on every test for the rest of the year. What I did not know was that he reached out to the 10th grade Math and Biology teachers who would become my teachers the next year. They turned a lost and hopeless kid into one with a plan to go to college. I even told my parents that I wanted to go to college. I was told no one in this family including extended family had ever gone to college. When I turned eighteen, I was expected to pay rent or I would be kicked out. My father wasn't finished. He said I was too stupid and would not make it. I responded to my father that I would either get a scholarship or work two jobs if that is what it would take.

High school went fast. I attended many funerals of friends. They were due to car wrecks, drug overdoses, shootings - even one by police during a robbery and another returning from Vietnam in a box. A neighbor was the one who took me for my driver's license test. When I took my SAT's I scored really well. The school counselor thought I had cheated, so I was told I needed to retake them at another school where they could ensure that I did not cheat. I scored even higher. To the surprise of everyone I knew (except a few teachers), I started engineering school completely paid for by scholarship and government grants. I finished one year when I received my draft notice in the summer before my second year was to start. This meant I would lose my scholarship, grants and opportunity for completing Engineering School. I decided to enlist in the Air Force and proceeded to basic training followed by technical school. It was early 1973 and I'm waiting for orders. Well, thirty-eight out of forty air-to-air missile airmen would get orders for Vietnam and Thailand.

If someone had told me that an all loving God in His infinite wisdom decided that my life and all the circumstances would ultimately be for my benefit, **my response at that time would have been: "He's doing a Really Shitty Job"!** We all have a story and millions had it better than I did. However, many more millions had it a lot worse. It is natural for humans to ask the question as to whether or not God is unjust or unfair. I, too, had that thought. Raising the question of unfairness assumes that I know what fairness is in its final, absolute sense. Since I do not know the mind of God, or what His plans are - except for what He would one day reveal to me from His Word - I see and experience only pieces. God sees the whole. When things seem to go sideways, I have to learn to trust Him. I would have to give up my right to know why. I was not there yet.

## SOVEREIGNTY OF GOD

### How does God's Sovereignty work according to God's Word?

Each of us had no say in being born. The how, where, why of our birth is not in our control. God's Word states that God is sovereign and is in control of everything. God's providence exists due to His sovereignty. He directs, regulates and governs every action in His universe, which includes every creature, by His completely wise and holy providence. He has the right to create or dispose of His creatures as He sees fit or pleases. He has the power to apply His knowledge so that the best possible purposes and outcomes are realized. God always does the right thing, at the right time and in the right way. God's general providence has to deal with the running of the universe. God's particular providence deals with the details of man's life. Since God knows all things, He then knows how to help His creatures to, as it says in Acts 17:27, PERHAPS seek Him, choose Him and - most importantly - know and serve Him. D.S Clarke states it this way: "The doctrine of God's sovereignty is a most helpful and encouraging doctrine. If we had our choice, which should we choose – to be governed by blind fate, or capricious chance, or irrevocable natural law, or a shortsighted and perverted self, or a mighty God infinitely wise, holy, loving and powerful? ***He who rejects God's sovereignty may take his choice with what is left.***"[2]

Sovereignty means God uses the acts of men to accomplish His Will. It also means that God uses His natural laws to accomplish His will. Some illustrations of God's Sovereignty will help us understand His power and control whether it is a person, a nation or His people.

## Great Britain needed God's Providence in 1588

Listen to the details of this famous battle that our generation's history books no longer include. In 1588, Phillip II of Spain sent the Spanish Armada to bring England back under the domination of the Holy Roman Catholic Church. England, being the first nation to break from the yoke of deception, would become the papacy's first example of the price paid for rebellion. The united power of the Papacy could easily crush England.

The Spanish fleet sailed up the English Channel to be met by a much smaller English Navy. The English had no hope. All over England the people had been fasting and praying for deliverance. The battle was on. The English ships paled in size, number, and power. The Spanish Armada expected to end this quickly. As the battle raged, the English Navy was throwing everything it had at the superior Spanish forces when

---

[2] Knowing The Doctrines of the Bible, Myer Pearlman, 1937, p 63

it became apparent they would run out of munitions much too soon. This is when God decides it is time to intervene, when all knew that only God's intervention would save them. A mighty storm arose, which blew the Spanish ships up against the coast of Holland, causing many to sink. The smaller English ships were able to maneuver during the storm, setting most of the Spanish ships on fire. A few Spanish ships limped home. Both England and those from Holland who witnessed the event, acknowledged the hand of God was present. In commemoration of the battle, they minted a coin. On the front side it showed Spanish ships sinking, on the back side men on their knees in prayer with the inscription: "Man Proposeth, God Disposeth," and the date "1588."

## Israel Needed God's Providence October 8, 1973

God's providence would be needed to save Israel. The Yom Kippur War should have been the annihilation of the state of Israel. Yom Kippur in Hebrew means "Day of Atonement." On the Day of Atonement, everything shuts down from two hours before sunset until two hours after the succeeding sunset. It is spent in prayer and fasting at home or in the synagogue. The Israeli military left only a token force at its borders. The Arabs were so soundly beaten in 1967 that Israel was quite confident that they had learned their lesson. *Apparently not!*

Syria had over 1200 tanks along the Golan Heights, a twenty-mile front. Egypt had another 3,000 tanks, 2,000 heavy guns, 1,000 aircraft and 600,000 men. The greatest tank battle in history would be fought in the Sinai on October 19th. Russia had provided both countries with many of their latest and most advanced weapons. Three days before the war started, Russia launched two Sputniks to insure that Israel could be watched. Due to Russian aerial intel, the start of the war was moved up four hours. The Egyptian plan was to take the Bar-Lev line in fifteen hours; they did it in five hours and then **they stopped**. The Syrians came to within one mile of Israel's Golan Heights. **They stopped**. Israel lost three of every five aircraft. Whole companies were completely wiped out.

Israel's Golan Heights Headquarters had only two tanks and ten men. At 7:00 am that morning, the Israel Defense Force started to recall troops on leave. This is why the war started at 2:00 pm instead of 6:00 pm as originally planned. It takes Israel at least 48 hours for a full mobilization. Time is what they needed. Israel was ready for the taking. Why had Syria and Egypt **stopped**? On November 5, 1973, a few days before the cease fire, a miracle happened: the chief Rabbi called Israel to prayer. That was the first official day of prayer that modern Israel ever had. The synagogues were packed and the Western wall was standing room only. A few weeks after the war Golda Meir said this: "For the first time in our twenty-five year history, we thought we might have lost." They knew they should have been destroyed. God's Sovereignty and Providence were on display once again!

## America Needed God's Providence July 9, 1755

Young Colonel Washington, along with a little more than one hundred Virginia provincials, was marching with General Braddock's twelve hundred plus British regulars. The destination was Fort Duquesne (Pittsburgh). The French, Canadians, and Indians had managed to assemble only eight hundred and fifty-five men. The French knew they would be no match for the British. They decided on an ambush seven miles from the fort. The battle plan was perfect. The British lines were stretched out over a few miles with the heavy artillery almost forty miles back. The Indians, being familiar with the territory, knew exactly the best location to ambush Braddock. Colonel Gage commanded the forward attachment with three hundred and fifty regulars and another two hundred and fifty ax men making a road. Suddenly, a storm of bullets showered down on them from the trees on both sides. Musket balls continued in waves from every direction inflicting extensive damage on Gage's troops. Braddock, hearing Gage was engaged with the French, moved the main body quickly toward Gage's position. Unfortunately, Gage's men broke and retreated in full stride colliding with Braddock's advancing troop. Confusion reigned. The British were at a loss on how to fight an enemy who would not show themselves. The Virginia provincials knew to take cover, but they would leave this place with only about thirty men. Captain Peyrouny and all of his officers perished. The highest-ranking provincial left, other than Washington, had a rank of corporal. Washington would ride the field carrying the general's orders during this two-hour period of sheer pandemonium. General Braddock and Colonel Gage were both killed. A total of seven hundred and fourteen soldiers were killed and/or seriously wounded. Eighty-six of this incredible number were officers. The British hastily retreated. Instead of pursuing them and finishing them, the victors go crazy in celebration, getting their scalps and booty.

After the battle George Washington records in a letter to his brother: "...I have been protected beyond all human probability or expectation; for I had four bullets through my coat, and two horses shot under me, yet escaped unhurt, although death was leveling my companions on every side of me!"

In 1770, while passing back through Western Pennsylvania fifteen years after the battle, George Washington - along with his traveling companion and lifelong friend Dr. Craik - are met by the Great Chief who was in charge of the July 9, 1755 ambush. Washington and Dr. Craik, through an interpreter, are told the following: "I am a chief and ruler over my tribes. My influence extends to the waters of the great lakes and to the far Blue Mountains. I have traveled a long and weary path that I might see the young warrior of the great battle. It was a day when white man's blood mixed with the streams of our forest that I first beheld this chief [Washington]. I called to my young men and said, mark yon tall and daring warrior. He is not of the redcoat tribe - he hath an Indian's wisdom, and his warriors fight as we do - himself is alone exposed. Quick, let your aim be certain, and he dies. ***Our rifles were leveled, rifles which, but for you, knew not how to miss – 'twas all in vain, a power far mightier than we, shielded him from harm. He [Washington] cannot die in battle..."*** Eighty years after the battle, a gold seal of Washington containing his initials, was found on the battlefield. A bullet had shot it off him.

## Slavery needed God's Man of Providence

Great Britain was so highly elevated to a point by God's providence that it would be known as "The Empire on which the Sun never set." Britain's Empire literally went around the globe, as did their Christian missionaries. Today, the international language is English, not because of America, but because of Britain. There is one very important fact about

Britain that most folks are not aware. The British Empire was deeply impacted by Christianity. One of the world's most influential Christians was William Wilberforce. Born in 1759, he served in Parliament from 1780 to 1825. He felt his calling to serve God was in politics. The first time he introduced an anti-slavery motion was in the House of Commons in 1788. In a three and one half hour oration, he concluded with the following: "Sir, when we think of eternity and the future consequences of all human conduct, what is there in life that shall make any man contradict the dictates of his conscience, the principles of justice and the *law of God*." The motion was defeated. However, he brought it up for the next eighteen years until the slave trade was abolished in 1806. He continued the campaign until a bill was passed abolishing slavery in the British territories on July 29, 1833. Four days later, he passed away. A year later, on July 31, 1834, approximately 800,000 slaves, mainly in the British West Indies, were set free.

The first two illustrations show that God's will determines the outcomes of battles, and which nations will be raised and which are to be punished. The next illustration of divine protection was extreme and well documented. This divine protection goes on daily. The final illustration is an example of God's will to remove one of man's curses. To accomplish this, He placed a burden upon one man to do a great task. The Bible reveals the truth about the God of this universe. Before creation, God states that He had a plan and that He predestined many things. The plan God has made was not made because of His foreknowledge but because of His goodness and perfect love. We will continue to explore more on predestination, election and the elect.

## Chapter 2

# PREDESTINED

The Bible clearly talks about predestination. What has God predestined according to His Word, and how does it affect my life? God's clearly states that, before creation, He knew each one of us. He tells us that He predestined the course of history. He shows us in His Word that the fate of nations are determined by Him, with consideration given for their actions. He has a plan for His creation. When there was a rebellion in heaven God was not caught off guard. Before Adam and Eve ate from the Tree of Knowledge He had a redemptive plan. God removed them from paradise, not because they disobeyed, but to prevent them from eating from the Tree of Life and thus obtaining eternal life.

Part of predestination involves God's Plan of Redemption, not only for His children, but His entire universe and all creation. Scripture clearly reveals that God's central and key player in redemption is Christ Jesus. God's redemption of humans starts off with a promise:

- Genesis 3:14-15: "So the LORD God said to the serpent, 'Because you have done this, cursed are you above all livestock and all wild animals! You will crawl on your belly and you will eat dust all the days of your life. And I will put enmity between you and the woman, and between your offspring and hers; he will crush your head, and you will strike his heel.'"

Satan, the master of deception and temptation, is punished and told that Christ will crush his head. This was accomplished at the cross.

God's Plan includes the calling of Abraham "The father of faith." God reveals to us that He calls many to carry out His will. Predestination is so important because God's Word reveals to us that it has a practical purpose. When God elected/called Jeremiah to do His will, He knew that Jeremiah was going to have a very difficult task and might be tempted to give up. So, God assures Jeremiah:

- <u>Jeremiah 1:5</u>: "Before I formed you in the womb I knew you, before you were born I set you apart; I appointed you as a prophet to the nations."

God tells Jeremiah that He knows what is coming and He will give Jeremiah the will and grace to accomplish what His will demands. This is true for each of us. When the New Testament describes Christians as objects of His foreknowledge, it reassures us that God knows what is coming and He has a plan for us. God's Word tells us that God promises help with our daily life, including our troubles/problems and dealing with temptations.

- <u>1 Corinthians 10:13</u>: "No temptation has overtaken you except what is common to mankind. And God is faithful; he will not let you be tempted beyond what you can bear. But when you are tempted, he will also provide a way out so that you can endure it."

God uses election. He selected Israel and the Jewish people as the "Chosen One." God's reason is that, from them, God's redemption would come. Scripture's revelation of God's plan is progressive over time. God made binding covenants with His people - that He would bless them and that the Messiah would come from their lineage. As you read the Scriptures, you will see God working through divinely selected people, nations and events. God shows His power and protection time and time again. Pick any person and/or event: Noah, Joseph, Moses, Pharaoh, Joshua, David, Solomon, (Shadrach, Meshach and Abednego), Nebuchadnezzar, Cyrus, etc. and what do you see? God at work.

Before time, God knew that Christ would come to earth as a result of a virgin birth and He would be born in a manger. Mary consents and is honored to be the mother of the "Son of God." Jesus would be 100% God and 100% human, thus another of His titles is "Son of Man." He would be tempted in all ways, yet remain the perfect sinless sacrifice - "The Lamb of God." Christ would give His life as payment for the disobedience of man. Adam's disobedience condemned all men to death. Christ's perfect obedience to God's will, His death on the cross and His victory over death provided redemption to all humans. The Bride of Christ is made up by the elect. Who are they? They are those who chose to bend their knee to God and chose to serve the invisible God who created them. God's Word tells us that God will judge all by the light they had and what choice they made. The New Testament tells us that the Bride includes His Church made up of the saints of God. They come from many different places and denominations. All have one thing in common: they have chosen, with their God-given free will, to accept God's provision for salvation, which is to respond to the wooing (drawing, calling, tugging) of the Holy Spirit.

Predestination, election and the elect are clearly in the Bible. What was predestined is taken from Scripture. Simply, The Bride of Christ. Redemption of God's creation cost God His most precious Son, Jesus. Why did He do it? His Goodness, Love, Grace and Mercy were directed toward us since before time. (Note below that He chose **us** plural not me singular or individually before time.)

- Ephesians 1:3-14: "Praise be to the God and Father of our Lord Jesus Christ, who has blessed *us* in the heavenly realms with every spiritual blessing in Christ. For he chose *us* in him before the creation of the world to be holy and blameless in his sight. **In love he predestined *us* for adoption to sonship through Jesus Christ**, in accordance with his pleasure and will—to the praise of his glorious grace, which he has freely given *us* in the One he loves. In him *we* have redemption through his blood, the forgiveness of sins, in accordance with the riches of God's grace that he lavished on *us.* With all wisdom and understanding, he made known to *us* the mystery of his will according to his good pleasure, which he purposed in Christ, to be put into effect when the times reach their fulfillment—to bring unity to all things in heaven and on earth under Christ. **In him *we* were also chosen,**

> *having been predestined according to the plan of him who works out everything in conformity with the purpose of his will*, in order that <u>*we*</u>, who were the first to put our hope in Christ, might be for the praise of his glory. And you also were *included in Christ when you heard the message of truth, the gospel of your salvation.* <u>*When you believe*</u>d, you were marked in him with <u>*a seal*</u>, the promised Holy Spirit, who is a deposit guaranteeing our inheritance until the redemption of those who are God's possession—to the praise of his glory."

God, in love, predestined <u>*us*</u> (the Bride of Christ) for **SALVATION** *before time.* He works out His Plan according to His Will, which was for the benefit of those who, when they heard the message of truth, believed and received the Holy Spirit - the Seal of God - as a deposit until all of God's promises are fulfilled at a future time known only to Him. I AM, Therefore I Know.

## Chapter 3

# FREE WILL

God is the cause of the _**fact**_ of free will - it was predestined by God before time. Humans are the causes of the _**acts**_ of free will. We have been given by God the right to be the first cause of our actions. This simply means we were not created as automatons, but in the image of God. We are able to make moral judgements of right and wrong, along with sorting out shades of gray.

One of God's important predestination decisions is known as the Bride of Christ. Take notice that this predestined election is corporate. This means what God predestined would be a Bride made up of the Elect. This was not an individual election - just like the predestined universal church was a corporate election, and not individuals. God knows who the elect are because He is the "I AM." Humans think in time and would naturally take God's Word and understand it from a limited vantage point.

- <u>1 Peter 1:1-2</u>: "Peter, an apostle of Jesus Christ, To God's elect, exiles scattered throughout the provinces of Pontus, Galatia, Cappadocia, Asia and Bithynia, **_who have been chosen according to the foreknowledge of God the Father,_** through the sanctifying work of the Spirit, to be obedient to Jesus Christ and sprinkled with his blood: Grace and peace be yours in abundance."

God does not use foreknowledge because He actually knows all. Any event, any person, the elect, and election are predetermined from the standpoint of God's omniscience. That same event and person is open and free from the vantage point of the human perspective and understanding. The two opposing concepts are complementary and coexist with both being true. God knows, humans must choose!

The question then arises: Do we have free will to do whatever we want? The answer is simply Yes or No. God's Sovereign Will comes first, our will comes second. When God's Word states that He is Love, that applies all the time to all of His creation. Tomorrow He cannot change and say hate is good and love is bad. Why? Because it comes from His unchangeable nature. He states that humans have been given limited free will. Limited because it is subject to His Will and the good plans He has for His creation. There are many examples in Scripture that we can review.

## PHARAOH OF EGYPT

Moses tells the Pharaoh of Egypt that he needs to set God's people free. Pharaoh says no. Scripture says that Pharaoh hardened his heart. When Pharaoh refused, this became a battle of gods. Egypt, like most ancient nations, was a nation of polytheism (many gods). Israel was an oddity, being a nation of monotheism, or a single God. This became evident when Moses' staff became a snake and ate the Egyptian magicians' two staffs, which turned into snakes.

- Exodus 7:9-12: "When Pharaoh says to you, 'Perform a miracle,' then say to **Aaron, 'Take your staff and throw it down before Pharaoh,' and it will become a snake."** So Moses and Aaron went to Pharaoh and did just as the Lord commanded. Aaron threw his staff down in front of Pharaoh and his officials, and it became a snake. Pharaoh then summoned wise men and sorcerers, and the Egyptian magicians also did the same things by their secret arts: Each one threw down his staff and it became a snake. ***But Aaron's staff swallowed up their staffs.***"

The message was clear, the cobra snake was the symbol of the ruling class. In fact, the crown of a pharaoh had the head of a cobra, ready to strike. When Moses destroyed their snakes, it meant that the true God was going to overcome the pharaoh's power. The battle between Israel's God and the gods of Egypt had begun!

**Plague One: The Nile River turns into Blood.** This miracle was against the god Hapi, the giver of life by flood, thus fertilizing the land and the god Hatmeyt, the fish god who was helpless to stop the fish from dying. (Exod. 7:14-25).

**Plague Two: Frogs.** Heqet, the frog-headed god was head of Egypt's oldest fertility cult. She was unable to stop the multiplication of the frogs (Exod. 8:1-15).

**Plague Three: Lice.** There is no known record of a lice god. However, Pharaoh's magicians informed Pharaoh that this "is the finger of God" (Exod. 8:16-19).

Something happens here that is recorded clearly in Exodus. God hardened Pharaoh's heart. It does not tell us exactly why God does it. However, Pharaoh's magicians tell Pharaoh that the third plague "is the finger of God." Scripture tells us that God would do seven additional plagues. At the end of this epic struggle, God's people would be released. God's Will was to publicly destroy the Egyptian gods and show the world His power.

- Romans 9:15-18: "For he says to Moses, 'I will have mercy on whom I have mercy, and I will have compassion on whom I have compassion.' *For Scripture says to Pharaoh: 'I raised you up for this very purpose, that I might display my power in you and that my name might be proclaimed in all the earth.'*"

Therefore, God has mercy on whom He wants to have mercy, and He hardens whom he wants to harden. God's Will is quite clear. Pharaoh's will is in subjection to God's Will.

**Plague Four: Flies (Beetles, Insects).** This was meant to be an affront to the god Khephera. This scarab-headed god under Ra was known as the fly-god who was related to sorcery. Soldiers wore a golden fly pin as a sign of bravery (Exod. 8:20-32).

**Plague Five: Murrain, or Anthrax.** This attacked the bull god Apis, the sacred cattle of Hathor, the cow-headed love goddess. Murrain or anthrax is an infectious disease that attacks cows. It is a form of skin cancer and can be transferred to humans. This attack was against Pharaoh who worshipped Hathor. (Exod. 9:1-7).

**Plague Six: Boils.** This plague was directly against the gods of healing, called Im-Hotep and the goddess Sekhet. Both were helpless to assist the Egyptians (Exod. 9:8-12).

**Plague Seven: Hail.** Nut was the sky goddess. She was the mother of the sun god Ra. The other gods that were called on would have been Resphu, Qetesh, and Set (supposed to be in charge of the winds and storms). Exodus 9:31 mentions that the flax and barley crops were destroyed.

**Plague Eight: Locusts.** Senehem was the locust-headed god. The locusts were so thick that the earth was darkened. By causing darkness while the sun was shining, Ra was discredited (Exod. 10:1-20).

**Plague Nine: Darkness.** The greatest god was the sun god, Amon Ra. He made possible all growth in humans, animals, and plants. After three days of darkness, their god Ra was scorned (Exod. 21:27).

**Plague Ten: Death of the First-Born.** Pharaohs were considered divine and Ra, the sun god, second. This plague was directed specifically against the Pharaoh and the future, his son. The Pharaoh who had to deal with Moses and Aaron was Amen-hotep II (Exod. 10:21-29).

It was necessary for God to harden Pharaoh's heart because God knew that Pharaoh could concede after any of these major defeats he suffered by the invisible and all powerful God of this universe. It was important that Israel be freed and Passover be established. This is one of the most important Jewish annual festivals. This meant God, in His omniscience, overrode man's will.

## EGYPTIANS

- Exodus 12:31-36: "During the night Pharaoh summoned Moses and Aaron and said, "Up! Leave my people, you and the Israelites! Go, worship the LORD as you have requested. Take your flocks and herds, as you have said, and go. And also bless me." The Egyptians urged the people to hurry and leave the country. "For otherwise," they said, "we will all die!" So the people took their dough before the yeast was added, and carried it on their shoulders in kneading troughs wrapped in clothing. The Israelites did as Moses instructed and asked the Egyptians for articles of silver and gold and for clothing. ***The LORD had made the Egyptians*** *favorably disposed toward the people, and they gave them what they asked for, so they plundered the Egyptians."*

Here God's Will is that all the Egyptians will freely give the Israelites their wealth/treasure. God is able to compel/influence them in spite of the fact that each family had just lost their firstborn. The masters were helping their former slaves. The free will of this whole nation submitted to the sovereign Will of God.

## JOB

The story of Job teaches us again about the sovereignty of God's Will and the creation of free will.

- Job 1:6-12: "One day the angels came to present themselves before the LORD, and Satan also came with them. The LORD said to Satan, 'Where have you come from?' Satan answered the LORD, 'From roaming throughout the earth, going back and forth on it.' Then the LORD said to Satan, 'Have you considered my servant Job? There is no one on earth like him; he is blameless and upright, a man who fears God and shuns evil.' 'Does Job fear God for nothing?' Satan replied. 'Have you not put a hedge around him and his household and everything he has? You have blessed the work of his hands, so that his flocks and herds are spread throughout the land. But now stretch out your hand and strike everything he has, and **he will surely curse you to your face.'** The ***LORD said to Satan, 'Very well, then, everything he has is in your power, but on the man himself do not lay a finger.'*** Then Satan went out from the presence of the LORD."

Job's whole life is changed from being blessed to being cursed. Everything is removed and Satan does not lay a finger on Job. Job's response is found in

- Job 1:20-22: "At this, Job got up and tore his robe and shaved his head. Then he fell to the ground in worship and said: 'Naked I came from my mother's womb, and naked I will depart. The

LORD gave and the LORD has taken away; may the name of the LORD be praised.' In all this, **Job did not sin by charging God with wrongdoing.**"

Job's second test applied more pain.

- Job 2:3-7: "Then the LORD said to Satan, 'Have you considered my servant Job? *There is no one on earth like him; he is blameless and upright, a man who fears God and shuns evil.* And he still maintains his integrity, though you incited me against him to ruin him without any reason.' 'Skin for skin!' Satan replied. 'A man will give all he has for his own life. But now stretch out your hand and strike his flesh and bones, and he will surely curse you to your face.' The LORD said to Satan, *'Very well, then, he is in your hands; but you must spare his life.'* So Satan went out from the presence of the LORD and afflicted Job with painful sores from the soles of his feet to the crown of his head."

Job and his wife both have free will. Her advice: curse God and die. Let's see what Job does with his free will.

- Job 2:9-10: "His wife said to him, 'Are you still maintaining your integrity? *Curse God and die!'* He replied, 'You are talking like a foolish woman. Shall we accept good from God, and not trouble?'"

"In all this, Job did not sin in what he said." Job decided to be faithful and trust God.

- Job 13:15: *"Though he slay me, yet will I hope in him..."*

Job continues to question God as to why he is suffering. Job believes he deserves an answer.

- Job 38:4: God provides an answer: "Where were you when I laid the earth's foundation? Tell me, if you understand."

*I Am, Therefore I Know*

God's response continues for five chapters. Job repents and humbles himself before the Lord. The Lord then restores all that Job lost and more. We learn that God's Will is sovereign and Job had free will to respond in a sinful manner or not. Satan has limited free will. He, too, has freedom of choice but its limits are set by God's Sovereign Will. Satan was once Lucifer (literally, "the light bearer"). He was the most glorious of all the angels ever created. He wanted to be like God. In his rebellion he became Satan, which means adversary - a summation of what His goals are. With his free will he has tried to stop God's plan of redemption. Satan has already lost.

## ESAU & JACOB

Another narrative that shows God's sovereignty and man's free will working together is found in:

- Genesis 25:21-23: "Isaac prayed to the LORD on behalf of his wife, because she was childless. The LORD answered his prayer, and his wife Rebekah became pregnant. The babies jostled each other within her, and she said, 'Why is this happening to me?' So she went to inquire of the LORD. The LORD said to her, 'Two nations are in your womb, and two peoples from within you will be separated; one people will be stronger than the other, and the older will serve the younger.'"

God's Will is that the younger will rule over the older. Esau, the elder brother, returned from the open country famished one day. Jacob, the younger brother, had just prepared some stew. Esau implores Jacob to give him some. Jacob agrees under one condition.

- Genesis 25:31-33: "Jacob replied, 'First sell me your birthright.' 'Look, I am about to die,' Esau said. 'What good is the birthright to me?' But Jacob said, 'Swear to me first.' So he swore an oath to him, selling his birthright to Jacob."

Jacob with his mother's help decides to steal Esau's blessing. Rebekah gets Esau's clothes and puts them on Jacob. Esau has a hairy body so

Rebekah covered Jacob's hands and the smooth part of his neck with goat skins.

- Genesis 27:21-29: "Then Isaac said to Jacob, 'Come near so I can touch you, my son, to know whether you really are my son Esau or not.' Jacob went close to his father Isaac, who touched him and said, 'The voice is the voice of Jacob, but the hands are the hands of Esau.' He did not recognize him, for his hands were hairy like those of his brother Esau; so he proceeded to bless him. **'Are you really my son Esau?' he asked. 'I am,'** he replied. Then he said, 'My son, bring me some of your game to eat, so that I may give you my blessing.' Jacob brought it to him and he ate; and he brought some wine and he drank. Then his father Isaac said to him, 'Come here, my son, and kiss me.' So he went to him and kissed him. When Isaac caught the smell of his clothes, he blessed him and said, 'Ah, the smell of my son is like the smell of a field that the LORD has blessed. May God give you heaven's dew and earth's richness – an abundance of grain and new wine. May nations serve you and peoples bow down to you. **Be lord over your brothers,** and may the sons of your mother bow down to you. May those who curse you be cursed and those who bless you be blessed.'"

This blessing of Isaac cannot be undone. Rebekah and Jacob have taken advantage of Isaac's old age and his poor eyesight. Here is the final announcement that Esau, father of the Edomites, will serve his younger brother.

- Genesis 27:36: "Esau said, 'Isn't he rightly named Jacob? This is the second time he has taken advantage of me: He took my birthright, and now he's taken my blessing!' Then he asked, 'Haven't you reserved any blessing for me?'

Esau gets one but it is not what he expected.

- Genesis 27:40: "You will live by the sword and you will serve your brother. But when you grow restless, you will throw his yoke from off your neck."

***God's will is served but it was accomplished by the evil actions of people.***

- Genesis 35:10-11: "God said to him, 'Your name is Jacob, but you will no longer be called Jacob; your name will be **Israel**.' And God said to him, 'I am God Almighty; be fruitful and increase in number. A nation and a community of nations will come from you, and **kings will be among your descendants**.'"

Jacob is renamed Israel and his lineage includes King David, Solomon and - *most importantly - the King of Kings: Christ Lord of All!*

## JOSEPH

Another famous narrative in Scripture describes the life of Joseph. Joseph's brothers decided to kill him. Instead, he is sold as a slave to an Egyptian caravan owner, since that brought them profit. Here is another plan of God that evil men execute.

- Genesis 39:1-4: "Now Joseph had been taken down to Egypt. Potiphar, an Egyptian who was one of Pharaoh's officials, the captain of the guard, bought him from the Ishmaelites who had taken him there. The LORD was with Joseph so that he prospered, and he lived in the house of his Egyptian master. When his master saw that the LORD was with him and that the LORD gave him success in everything he did, Joseph found favor in his eyes and became his attendant. Potiphar put him in charge of his household, and he entrusted to his care everything he owned."

Potiphar's wife wanted Joseph to sleep with her. When he refused she accused him of trying to rape her.

- Genesis 39:20-23: "Joseph's master took him and put him in prison, the place where the **king's prisoners** were confined. But while Joseph was there in the prison, the LORD was with him; he showed him kindness and granted him favor in the eyes of the prison warden. So the warden put Joseph in charge of all those

- Genesis 40:1-3: "Sometime later, the cupbearer and the baker of the king of Egypt offended their master, the king of Egypt. Pharaoh was angry with his two officials, the chief cupbearer and the chief baker, and put them in custody in the house of the captain of the guard, in the same prison where Joseph was confined."

They both have dreams and Joseph, with God's help, provides the cupbearer and baker with the interpretation. The chief cupbearer will be restored to his former position in three days. The chief baker finds out that Pharaoh will lift off his head and impale his body on a pole in three days. It happened exactly as Joseph said.

Pharaoh had a bad dream that no one was able to interpret. The chief cupbearer remembered Joseph had the ability to interpret dreams. Pharaoh had Joseph brought to him. Joseph states the dream means there are going to be seven years of abundance followed by seven years of severe famine.

- Genesis 41:39-41: "Then Pharaoh said to Joseph, 'Since God has made all this known to you, there is no one so discerning and wise as you. You shall be in charge of my palace, and all my people are to submit to your orders. Only with respect to the throne will I be greater than you.' So Pharaoh said to Joseph, 'I hereby put you in charge of the whole land of Egypt.'"

Why does God need Joseph in Egypt?

- Genesis 45:7-8: "**But God sent me ahead of you to preserve for you a remnant on earth and to save your lives by a great deliverance.** So then, **it was not you who sent me here, but God.** He made me father to Pharaoh, lord of his entire household and ruler of all Egypt."

Because of Joseph's interpretation of Pharoah's dreams, Egypt was the only country to store food. Joseph's family would have perished unless Joseph was in a position to do God's will and protect the holy lineage leading to Christ. Would it be unreasonable for Joseph to have thought: what in the world is God doing? After all, his brothers sold him into slavery. Then he was thrown into the king's prison. Again, God's Sovereign Will is being perfectly executed by imperfect humans with evil intentions. Yet, God is able to work it out according to His Plan which is for good. He is good not because of the things He does; He is good because that is who He is!

## MARY

Mary, the mother of Jesus, shows us that God is the ultimate respecter of human free will.

- <u>Luke 1:26-38</u>: "In the sixth month of Elizabeth's pregnancy, God sent the angel Gabriel to Nazareth, a town in Galilee, to a virgin pledged to be married to a man named Joseph, a descendant of David. The virgin's name was Mary. The angel went to her and said, 'Greetings, you who are highly favored! The Lord is with you.' Mary was greatly troubled at his words and wondered what kind of greeting this might be. But the angel said to her, ***Do not be afraid, Mary; you have found favor with God. You will conceive and give birth to a son, and you are to call him Jesus.*** He will be great and will be called the Son of the Most High. The Lord God will give him the throne of his father David, and he will reign over Jacob's descendants forever; his kingdom will never end.' 'How will this be,' Mary asked the angel, 'since I am a virgin?' The angel answered, ***The Holy Spirit will come on you,*** and the power of the Most High will overshadow you. So the holy one to be born will be called the Son of God. Even Elizabeth your relative is going to have a child in her old age, and she who was said to be unable to conceive is in her sixth month. For no word from God will ever fail.' ***'I am the Lord's servant,'*** Mary answered. ***'May your word to me be fulfilled.'*** Then the angel left her."

Reverend Edward E. Menaldino writes this profound insight about free will and faith: "Conception took place after the annunciation and Mary's acceptance of the proposal. 'Behold the handmaid of the Lord; be it unto me according to thy word.' To come upon her without consent would be rape. The announcement could not come after the fact. Though God is sovereign, **He functions within moral laws.** The sequence of events reveals the role of faith. Jesus' conception required a response of faith by Mary to the annunciation. She heard a promise, she believed the Word and Christ was born within her."[3] Mary heard, chose to believe, and exercised her free will by saying "yes" in faith. She could have said "no" which was her ***God-given, God-respected right of free will!***

## ESTHER

The story of Esther shows how God places people in perfect positions to do His Will. Mordecai comes to Esther knowing she is Queen.

- <u>Esther 4:14:</u> "For if you remain silent at this time, relief and deliverance for the Jews will arise from another place, but you and your father's family will perish. And who knows but that you have come to your royal position for such a time as this?"

The Jews have an enemy named Haman, who has convinced the king to wipe out all the Jews that are spread throughout his empire. The royal orders have been issued. Haman had a fifty foot pole set up for Mordecai's death outside his house. The plan is set. Esther knew that going to the king without being summoned could mean her death. Nevertheless, she does and the Jews are once again saved from annihilation. Haman ends up on the pole in front of his house.

## NATIONS

Free will also is applied to nations which are judged here and now by God. Listen to

---

[3] Parson to Person, Reverend Edward Menaldino, 2015, p 210

- Jeremiah 18:1-10: "This is the word that came to Jeremiah from the LORD: 'Go down to the potter's house, and there I will give you my message.' So I went down to the potter's house, and I saw him working at the wheel. But the pot he was shaping from the clay was marred in his hands; so the potter formed it into another pot, shaping it as seemed best to him. Then the word of the LORD came to me. He said, 'Can I not do with you, Israel, as this potter does?' declares the LORD. "Like clay in the hand of the potter, so are you in my hand, Israel. *If at any time I announce that a nation or kingdom is to be uprooted, torn down and destroyed, and if that nation I warned repents of its evil, then I will relent and not inflict on it the disaster I had planned. And if at another time I announce that a nation or kingdom is to be built up and planted, and if it does evil in my sight and does not obey me, then I will reconsider the good I had intended to do for it.*"

## JONAH

The story of Jonah is an example of a nation's free choice. Destruction or repentance!

- In Jonah 3:1-11: "Then the word of the LORD came to Jonah a second time: 'Go to the great city of Nineveh and proclaim to it the message I give you.' Jonah obeyed the word of the LORD and went to Nineveh. Now Nineveh was a very large city; it took three days to go through it. Jonah began by going a day's journey into the city, proclaiming, 'Forty more days and Nineveh will be overthrown.' The Ninevites believed God. A fast was proclaimed, and all of them, from the greatest to the least, put on sackcloth. When Jonah's warning reached the king of Nineveh, he rose from his throne, took off his royal robes, covered himself with sackcloth and sat down in the dust. This is the proclamation he issued in Nineveh: 'By the decree of the king and his nobles: Do not let people or animals, herds or flocks, taste anything; do not let them eat or drink. But let people and animals be covered with sackcloth. Let everyone call urgently on God. Let them give up their evil

ways and their violence. Who knows? God may yet relent and with compassion turn from his fierce anger so that we will not perish.'"
**When God saw what they did and how they turned from their evil ways, he relented and did not bring on them the destruction he had threatened.**

What is God's will for *"everyone"*? Jesus says it clearly in

- John 6:40: *"For my Father's will is that <u>everyone</u> who looks to the Son and believes in him shall have eternal life, and I will raise them up at the last day."*

Our limited free will must fit into God's Sovereign Will. How does God do this? First, He knows all. Second, He uses His unlimited knowledge, with power, to bring circumstances to bear. He opens doors and He places people according to His plans. He is able to guide us as we, with our free will, choose "right versus left" or "yes versus no." God's infinite wisdom and power work out all the details for our ultimate good. That good is that we "**PERHAPS**" come to know Him personally versus knowing about Him.

## Chapter 4

# WHOSOEVER

I felt extremely fortunate knowing that the foreign country I was going to spoke English. I arrived in early 1974 at RAF Bentwaters. After I landed in Great Britain, I got myself an MG sports car and it was "party time." Being drafted had removed any hope of finishing college at this time. That dream died as my father said it would. During this time, I worked at an explosive shop full of bombs and missiles. It is the building on a base that is farthest away from everyone else with the protection walls designed to keep an explosion from destroying the rest of the base. They showed us films of what happened in different explosive incidents. It was ugly. We almost had an incident. It was one of the scariest events that I was ever involved in. The next event that was to shake me to the core would happen about one month later.

    I was driving home on a small winding English road that I had driven many times before. I thought the road conditions were relatively safe. It was night, the temperature was just above freezing and I came upon some "black ice." As I came around the next curve my MG began to spin out. I jerked the wheel in the opposite direction, something broke in the steering column, and the car spun helplessly in the opposite direction. I knew this road, how it was tree-lined. I knew that, as my headlights moved around and around, it would only be a matter of time until ***I was going to die***. It was as if time stopped. My mind was running through many key events and relationships in my life; things became extremely vivid. I still remember this incident today with intense clarity. Suddenly the car came to rest. The steering column had broken, making it impossible to direct the car after the initial attempt. The realization of how utterly helpless I was during this near-death incident fell upon me like a load of bricks. Death came knocking at my door once again and I knew I was not ready. I had no idea of what life was really about. Just then an older man knocked on my window. As I wound down the window, all he could say was how did I do that? He said it was just incredible. As he left, I knew I had done squat. I couldn't have even if I wanted to. Circumstances had finally brought me to a point of decision in my life. It was then that I looked up into the heavens and said these words, "God, if you're there, I want to know you."

There was this guy at the missile shop on base whose name was Paul. He was different from all the rest of us. He seemed to have a peace about him that was almost unnerving. Paul was always in control, even though we would bust on him for being too nice of a person. Paul was self confident without being the least bit arrogant or having any evidence of self-pride. He had clarity of vision and was focused on accomplishing his goals. He had a great sense of humor and was easy to like. He was a hard worker and we were assigned to the same missile crew. I had not previously met anyone like him. Paul had asked me multiple times to a Bible study that he attended off base at a friend's home. Paul asked me once a week for probably three months and every week he got the same answer. This week it would be different. He told me there would be lots of home cooked food and desserts, which sounded great. The truth was I realized I could, and should, be dead.

When we arrived, there were about seventy-five folks gathered in the living room singing songs to their God. I sensed something I had never felt before. The following week Paul again asked me to come to their Bible study. This time I accepted more out of curiosity than anything else. I wanted to understand what these people had. This went on for about a month. Then Paul invited me to the base chapel for a Sunday evening service. I attended and many of the same folks I had met with Paul were there. They were all really accepting and concerned for me; yet, they had no reason. In my old neighborhood, where I grew up for all my nineteen years, we were rarely nice to anyone. These new people were strange. I said to myself "they would have never had a chance of survival in my old neighborhood." I now found myself attending the base chapel and their

Bible study on a regular basis. One thing I was getting was a lot of new information about their God.

The Bible study was from the Navigator's ministries and they started with the basics. I had not even heard this verse before:

- John 3:16-17 *"For God so loved the world that he gave his one and only Son, that whoever believes in him shall not perish but have eternal life. For God did not send his Son into the world to condemn the world, but to save the world through him."*

I did not even know that Jesus came to save the whole world. The object of God's love is the whole world; could that ever include me? I had some real qualification issues. I had done a lot of bad things in my life. When I was fourteen, my Dad broke my mother's collarbone during a drunken rage. When I found her I drove her to the hospital. The police asked who drove her in. I raised my hand. They just said don't ever do it again. This brings me to the last thing I did before leaving for England. I purposely came back home to make sure my Dad knew that if he ever touched anyone in the family again, I would come home and kill him. He never did after that threat because he knew I meant it.

The Bible study was in Romans. In the first chapter I found out what the Good News is.

- Romans 1:16-17: "For I am not ashamed of the gospel, because it is the **power of God that brings salvation to <u>everyone</u> who believes**: first to the Jew, then to the Gentile. For in the gospel the righteousness of God is revealed—a righteousness that is by faith from first to last, just as it is written: *'The righteous will live by faith.'*

The **Good News** is everyone who **believes by faith** can be saved.

- Ephesians 2:8-9 states: "For it is **by grace you have been saved, through faith** - and this is not from yourselves, it is the **gift of God - not by works**, so that no one can boast."

I had never heard this: that Salvation is by choosing to believe by faith, and salvation is a gift from God because of His freely given grace to us.

In Romans, the next truth revealed to me was the Bad News. God gives us knowledge of Him and it is clearly understood by us. God also writes his laws on our hearts.

- Romans 1:20: "For since the creation of the world God's invisible qualities—his eternal power and divine nature—have been clearly seen, being understood from what has been made, *so that people are without excuse*."

- Romans 2:14-15: "Indeed, when Gentiles, who do not have the law, do by nature things required by the law, they are a law for themselves, even though they do not have the law. They show that the requirements of the *law are written on their hearts,* their consciences also bearing witness, and their thoughts sometimes accusing them and at other times even defending them."

I chose idolatry, which means I rejected God and served this world (1:1-23). This leads to self-indulgence.

- Romans 1:28-32: "Furthermore, just as they did not think it *worthwhile to retain the knowledge of God*, so God gave them over to a depraved mind, so that they do what ought not to be done. They have become filled with every kind of wickedness, evil, greed and depravity. They are full of envy, murder, strife, deceit and malice. They are gossips, slanderers, God-haters, insolent, arrogant and boastful; they invent ways of doing evil; they disobey their parents; they have no understanding, no fidelity, no love, no mercy. *Although they know God's righteous decree* that those who do such things deserve death, they not only continue to do these very things but *also approve* of those who practice them."

I could not disagree with God's Word. It described most of the people on the street where I was raised. The Bad News concludes with a summary statement in

- Romans 3:10-11: "As it is written: ***There is no one righteous, not even one**; **there is no one who understands; there is no one who seeks God.***"

This was revealing to me. I thought that religious people were somewhat righteous. This was a lot to process. Not one person is righteous, all fall short, and salvation is a gift acquired by believing by faith and not on works?

Each week, as I continued going to Bible study, I would learn another truth. The next truth was about how God could justify me; someone who knew he was not righteous. I learned that justification is a legal term that means God declares someone righteous. It states that Christ's righteousness is imputed to those who believe by faith in the fact that Christ died on the cross and paid for the world's sins.

- Romans 3:22-28: "This righteousness is given through faith in Jesus Christ to all who believe. There is no difference between Jew and Gentile, ***for all have sinned*** and fall short of the glory of God, and ***all are justified freely by his grace*** through the redemption that came by Christ Jesus. God presented ***Christ as a sacrifice of atonement***, through the shedding of his blood—***to be received by faith.*** He did this to demonstrate his righteousness, because in his forbearance he had left the sins committed beforehand unpunished—he did it to demonstrate his righteousness at the present time, so as to be just and ***the one who justifies those who have faith in Jesus.*** Where, then, is boasting? It is excluded. Because of what law? The law that requires works? No, because of the law that requires faith. For we maintain that ***a person is justified by faith apart from the works of the law.***"

I believe all have sinned. After all, I was good at it and, hate to say, enjoyed it. Here we see that Christ's sacrifice is the payment for all sin: past, present and future. Another thing I found out was that Abraham was justified by faith. I thought the Israelites got their righteousness by observing the laws? Abraham is called the "Father of Faith." Abraham was even uncircumcised when God chose him.

- Romans 4:10-11: "Under what circumstances was it credited? **Was it after he** [Abraham added] **was circumcised, or before? It was not after, but before!** And he received circumcision as a sign, a seal of the righteousness that he had by faith while he was still uncircumcised. So then, **he is the father of all who believe** but have not been circumcised, in order that righteousness might be credited to them. **The law was given for one reason; to guarantee that all would see their need for the saving grace of Jesus.**"

I learned that God gave us the law for one purpose. To guarantee we would see that we are sinners and **PERHAPS** see our need for the saving grace of Jesus. God demonstrated His love towards us before we even understood our need for it, even though we rejected Him.

- Romans 5:8: "But God demonstrates his own love for us in this: **While we were still sinners, Christ died for us.** Since we have now been justified by his blood, how much more shall we be **saved from God's wrath through him**!"

I was hearing these truths but they were foreign to me. My mind remained stuck on why God does good to people who reject Him, and even use His Holy Name in vain? We also will be saved from God's wrath. It had never occurred to me that God was going to hold me accountable for my choices and, on top of that, punish me.

- Romans 5:17-18: "For if, by the trespass of the one man, death reigned through that one man, how much more will those who receive God's abundant provision of grace and of the gift of righteousness reign in life through the one man, Jesus Christ! **Consequently, just as one trespass resulted in condemnation for all people, so also one righteous act resulted in justification and life for all people.**"

Adam brought death. Jesus brought life for those who chose God's one provision for salvation. Week after week, I was learning new truths, such as I was a slave to my desires, wants and – as Scripture says – my sin.

*I Am, Therefore I Know*

I discovered who I truly served. It was the unholy trinity: "Me, Myself and I."

The Scriptures revealed to me that there is a choice."

- Romans 6:16-19: "Don't you know that when you offer yourselves to someone as obedient slaves, you are slaves of the one you obey—whether you are slaves to sin, which leads to death, or to obedience, which leads to righteousness? But thanks be to God that, though you used to be slaves to sin, you have come to obey from your heart the pattern of teaching that has now claimed your allegiance. **You have been set free from sin** and have become slaves to righteousness."

Scripture states that I, a former slave to sin, can - by choice - be freed from the bondage of sin. My first thought was: do I really want to be set free? And, why do it?

- Romans 6:23: *"For the wages of sin is death, but the gift of God is eternal life in Christ Jesus our Lord."*

God's Word clearly states that sin will bring death, followed by hell, which is pretty much what I deserved. Eternal life sounded better, but can't I have both – live my life, and accept Jesus just before I die?

Months had passed from my first night at Bible study. I had learned much about God, but I still did not know Him or if I could know Him. The next Sunday evening service we had a visiting English preacher from a local church, who was to be our guest speaker. That night as this Englishman spoke, it was as if he was speaking only to me. His voice sounded extremely powerful. Later I would come to understand that he was anointed (the speaker's power coming from the power of the Holy Spirit). He spoke with such clarity, authority, and conviction. His eyes seemed to look right into me. As he shared the love of God, and the simplicity of God's plan of salvation, I wondered why I never saw it before. It was as if my eyes had veils over them for the past few months. As he talked, he shared that God gave us the law out of His great love. He knew no one could ever keep it. This would make it obvious to all that they needed a Savior. God requires us to call upon the name of Jesus to be saved - you know, the "Repent and be Saved" deal. Accept God's provision, which was sending the Son of God to the cross to take my sin away. He explained how. It was too simple, which I believe is the reason I missed it. It was acquired by faith. Yet, most prefer some kind of works to be involved (I think having to do works was good for my pride. I could not believe something was actually free). As he finished up, he talked about what awaits someone who does not respond to God's call. It sent shivers down my spine. It was the first time in my life eternity came into clear focus. I needed to act upon what I sensed was fact and make it part of my life.

That night I returned home and, for the first time in my life, I considered bending my will to someone. My circumstances, relationships to people, and upbringing had forced me to become totally self-sufficient, where I relied on no one because people could not be counted on to keep their word. What was being asked was absolutely opposite of my whole mindset of distrust. I never needed anything from anyone. ***I had learned that no one else was going to help you.***

Now, my pride was on the line. Someone wanted to give me something for free. No one ever gave me anything for free. All I had to do was step out in faith. I walked into the bedroom and knelt down at the end of the bed. I began to talk to God (I did not know how to pray, so I talked). I repented of my ways, confessed my wrongdoings, and asked Christ to save me by faith. What happened next was the most incredible experience I have ever had.

In that instant, my heart changed, my feelings about people changed, a new love entered my heart that was unnatural, and I broke down in tears as God lifted the weight of sin and hopelessness from my inner being. The Holy Spirit had entered in by request and transformed me from top to bottom. I was not prepared for this. As I got up from the end of the bed I sensed my life would never be the same. I had no idea of how radical a change there would be. At the next Bible study, I shared with everyone what I had done. They were overjoyed and we all celebrated, which to me was still a new experience. I guess what attracted me most to these Christians was their genuine love for me, each other, and everyone they met.

I noticed changes that only confirmed that something real had happened. I was concerned that this step of faith was just emotion, but then the following desires disappeared: I did not want to go out to the clubs, did not want to chase women, stopped using foul language, and just wanted to read and learn all I could about God and His book, the Bible. What was going on?

I discovered whosoever meant me. I was one of the all. God had brought me thousands of miles to a foreign country from where I was raised, away from all my negative influences so that as his word says in Acts 16:27: **"PERHAPS** I would choose to serve Him."

After being in Christ for about six months, I decided to pray for a strong Christian wife. I did not have the gift of singleness and Scripture says "not to be unequally yoked." That prayer was Friday, July 4th 1975. Sunday night she was at the evening service and sat near me. I knew at that time she was not a believer. However, the Holy Spirit prompted me to ask her out. I did and our first informal date was that Tuesday. She made me lunch – shepherd's pie – which was delicious, and we played tennis. Our first official date was that Friday evening. I knocked on the door and her father opened the door and invited me in. I could not believe who it was! I had asked my commander's daughter out. Being smarter than I look, I asked him what time he would like his daughter home. He said 11:00 sharp! We went to Felixstowe on the southeast coast. She tried oxtail soup for the first time and really liked it. There was one thing she did not like and that was me taking her home at 10:15 pm. I told her to trust me on this one! Our next date was Bible Study. She, too, had circumstances in her life that He allowed so that, as it says in Acts 16:27 **"PERHAPS"** she would choose to serve Him, which she did.

## Chapter 5

# UNDERSTAND

What does it mean to be a Christian? We both had just entered into a new relationship with God. We received salvation. We believed that Christ was the only way to the Father.

- John 14:6: "Jesus answered, '*I am the way and the truth and the life.* No one comes to the Father except through me.'"

- John 3:3: "Jesus replied, 'Very truly I tell you, no one can see the kingdom of God unless they are born again.'"

Scripture tells us God loves us, which is why He gets angry. God's anger is a "Holy Anger" which comes from His perfect love for us. God's anger is with my sin and evil deeds. He knows that they harm us. I can be so cool in difficult situations, at work doing negotiations, giving advice when someone has slipped, or maneuvering through the many challenges we have to deal with daily. When it involves someone I care about and love, then I get emotional and even become angry. The more I love the person, the more it impacts my emotional state. Imagine God's perfect love for each of us. He hates our sin and what it would cost us, so He predestined the Cross!

It was His plan for Christ to conquer death for all who believe. God sends His Holy Spirit to draw all unto Christ. Salvation is an act of grace that was predestined from before time. God does all the work. Grace is not performance based. People desperately want to be accepted and loved.

Why the saying *"Dog, Man's Best Friend"?* It's because dogs give us what we secretly treasure more than anything, *"Unconditional Love."* Grace means we get God's unconditional love. *That means I cannot do anything to increase or decrease His love towards me.* He sees and loves me through Christ. We then receive God's unconditional love that we desperately want. *Each of us has a spiritual void that can only be filled by God.* Blaise Pascal, a French mathematician and philosopher, put it like this: "There is a God-shaped vacuum in the heart of every man which cannot be filled by any created thing, but only by God the Creator, made known through Jesus Christ."

My wife and I left for our honeymoon. We jumped in our car and spent the next three weeks driving throughout Northern Europe. On the inside of our wedding bands we had the verse from

- Mark 10:9: "What God has joined together let no man put asunder."

We made a commitment to each other and to God. We entered marriage by taking a vow for better, for worse and for life.

Did I understand what God had prepared for me? Not even close.

- Romans 8:15-17: "The Spirit you received does not make you slaves, so that you live in fear again; rather, the Spirit you received brought about *your adoption to sonship*. And by him we cry, 'Abba, Father.' The Spirit himself testifies with our spirit that we are God's children. Now if we are children, then we are heirs— *heirs of God and co-heirs with Christ*, if indeed we share in his sufferings in order that we may also share in his glory."

Without realizing it, I had entered into another intimate relationship best described as a marriage. I made a vow to serve Christ. I had become part of His Bride, one of the elect. Just like my marriage to my wife, *it started with the commitment to love with mutual interdependence, a dreamy future together.* Then we realize that this oath we made will help us through the laborious and real task of living together. I enter a similar type of relationship with Christ. I have to live out my life in relationship to being in Christ, part of His Bride. We are told we are children, then heirs, not just any kind of heirs but God's heirs and we are joint heirs with Christ. Game Changer! My total status changed. God is so intimate that I call out to him Abba which means "Daddy." It does not stop there.

- <u>Romans 8:26-27</u>: "In the same way, the Spirit helps us in our weakness. **We do not know what we ought to pray for**, but the Spirit himself intercedes for us through wordless groans. And he who searches our hearts knows the mind of the Spirit, because the **Spirit intercedes for God's people in accordance with the will of God**."

When God gave us the Holy Spirit; one of His jobs was to help and teach us how to pray. The best part, it states, is that I do not know how to pray according to God's will. My prayers are corrected by the Holy Spirit before being delivered to God. All prayers are heard and answered according to God's sovereign Will. The Holy Spirit in me is there for one sole reason, my benefit!

- <u>Romans 8:28-32</u>: *"**And we know that all things work together for good to them that love God, to them who are the called according to his purpose**. For whom he did foreknow, he also did predestinate to be conformed to the image of his Son, that he might be the firstborn among many brethren. Moreover whom he did predestinate, them he also **called:** and whom he called, them he also **justified:** and whom he justified, them he also **glorified**. What shall we then say to these things? **If God be for us, who can be against us?** He that spared not his own Son, but delivered him up for us all, how shall he not with him also freely give us all things?*

God is not going to hold back anything I will need to serve Him and to do His will. All things will be orchestrated by God; this means even the seemingly unimportant details. How? That is unknown to humans.

- <u>Romans 8:38-39</u>: "Who shall separate us from the love of Christ? Shall trouble or hardship or persecution or famine or nakedness or danger or sword? As it is written: 'For your sake we face death all day long; we are considered as sheep to be slaughtered.' No, in all these things we are more than conquerors through him who loved us. *For I am convinced that neither death nor life, neither angels nor demons, neither the present nor the future, nor any powers, neither height nor depth, nor anything else in all creation, will be able to separate us from the love of God that is in Christ Jesus our Lord."*

God has promised that no one has the power to remove us from His love.

- <u>Acts 4:8-13</u>: "Then Peter, **filled with the Holy Spirit**, said to them: 'Rulers and elders of the people! If we are being called to account today for an act of kindness shown to a man who was lame and are being asked how he was healed, then know this, you and all the people of Israel: It is by the name of Jesus Christ of Nazareth, whom you crucified but whom God raised from the dead, that this man stands before you healed. Jesus is "the stone you builders rejected, which has become the cornerstone." Salvation is found in no one else, for there is no other name under heaven given to mankind by which we must be saved. *When they saw the courage of Peter and John and realized that they were <u>unschooled, ordinary men,</u> they were astonished and they took note that these men had been with Jesus.*"

Is man able to live and/or die for the sake of his ideals and values without assistance? As an example, Peter denied Christ three times when his beliefs were tested. The disciples scattered in fear when Christ was arrested. As I read the Bible and books such as <u>Foxe's Book of Martyrs</u>, I knew the power, the courage and resolve the disciples had were beyond human capability. Before I got married, my best man and I searched the Scriptures for the secret of their strength, unbelievable courage and power. We were unable to figure it out.

One Sunday after service as I was standing with my wife. I heard the woman behind me say "My niece got saved and received the Baptism of the Holy Spirit while I was stateside." I immediately turned to her and introduced myself and my wife. I asked her if she understood the Baptism of the Holy Spirit and how to receive power like the disciples had in the book of Acts. She said yes, and asked if we would like to come over to her house that following Tuesday night to talk more about it? I knew that I needed this power to be able to witness. I had not witnessed to anyone out of fear and concern that I would not have the correct words. I was just like Peter before he received the power of the Holy Spirit at Pentecost.

Tuesday night we arrived. She opened the Scriptures and carefully explained to us that the Holy Spirit was able to supernaturally provide any believer who wanted and needed the Baptism of the Holy Spirit for the sole purpose of serving God. A funny thing happened when we prayed to receive this. I, who had been searching for months would receive it second to my wife, who had not sought it until that night. ***Our Baptisms were the same, but different. Same in purpose, same in power, but given with the Divine understanding of who we were.***

My best man got orders to leave and my orders stated that I would be honorably discharged October of 1976, returning back to my parent's home in the old neighborhood until employment could be found. God knew in less than two months I was going home and would need His power. Suddenly, I understood the need of God's Power to do His Work. Scripture tells us that when you are brought before anyone, do not be concerned with what to say. God's Holy Spirit will guide your words with power. God had prepared me to go back home with my new bride.

I shared with my wife many of the stories about growing up. By the time I was finished telling each story, we would be laughing because each tragedy was shared with the emphasis on what was humorous in the event. For example, for fun, one evening when I was in my early teens we decided to measure the height of the police car's new roof lights. We wanted to see if the reputation of the Keystone cops was real. It was dark and we created a ruckus near the chief of police's house. Of course, the police responded. As they drove down the street, their siren and lights were ripped off by a steel cable we had stretched between two telephone poles at our carefully measured height. Over ten of us were up in the two trees next to the crime. We watched as the police proved they were indeed members of the famous Keystone cops. To find us all they had to do was shine their flashlights up into the trees. Instead, they fruitlessly searched below. The White Van Story which we laugh about today, wasn't so funny the day it happened. One of my cousins stole the white van from the factory across the street from my house. The next day he told my brother and me about it. We decided to take it out for a joy ride with him. My cousin had hidden it down at the creek. When we arrived at the van, the police, who were waiting, started coming to get us. Escaping meant running across a field of sticker bushes in short pants, since it was summer, to get to the woods. The police did not follow, but they watched as we bloodied our legs during our escape. This time they got the laughs!

I knew that my family and all my former friends could no longer be my inner circle. God showed me they were my mission field. Whoever God brought into my life was for a purpose. Everyone had heard I was back and that I was "different". They came to see and hear what changed. They found out that I had accepted Christ as my Savior, and would no longer be participating in certain activities. When they saw my wife, they immediately came to the conclusion that I did it to get her. When I shared that I became a Christian before my wife did, they were mystified. Their brains could not grasp that someone would accept Christ without getting something out of it. I received so much more that they did not see or understand. My wife could not believe all the nicknames: Muskrat and Fat Pat, to name a couple. Where she came from people used their real first names. My wife went around the corner to my cousin's house and, when she returned, she was upset with me. I asked her what had happened? She told me that my cousin asked her what was wrong with me? My cousin told her that I had been home ten days and had not beaten anyone up. My wife responded to her that I do not beat people up. My cousin, and those who with her, chuckled upon hearing this. My wife then asked me the question upon returning home, "Did you beat people up?" When I smiled big, she knew. Then she said, "I thought your stories were funny and embellishments. Now I see they were all real. You did not tell me the half of it."

My best man contacted us just before we left England to tell us that he had the gotten the Baptism of the Holy Spirit. He then shared he found a good church that believed in the power of the Baptism of the Holy Spirit - Assembly of God. When we arrived back in the United States, we looked up an Assembly of God church for the closest one to my parents' home.

The first Sunday home we attended an Assembly of God church. Five Sundays later, we were at Sunday night service with the pastor praying over us while the whole congregation surrounded us. The Pastor prayed that we both would find employment. A man at the end came up and handed me his business card and said "call this person." I went to the job interview and got hired by the head of the four divisions of an automotive parts remanufacturing plant. He would set my starting hourly rate, and I would meet with him at the end of each week to assess my progress. My first day proved to be quite interesting. Having an electronics background, I started in the armature repair department. I did sixty-three repairs with no rejects. The next day I was confronted by the department bully who set the unofficial repair and rejection rate. He told me it was to be thirty with three rejects. I did seventy plus every day that first week. At the end of the month, I was Department Manager. Eighteen months later I was the Plant Manager for the Master Cylinders Division.

My wife gave me a plaque inscribed with:

- <u>Jeremiah 29:11</u>: **"For I know the plans I have for you," declares the LORD, "plans to prosper you and not to harm you, plans to give you hope and a future."**

It was God's promise and we still have it, decades later. As noted previously, Joseph's success was because of God. We believed the same thing. We were learning to put our trust in God. One Sunday morning there was a request to give for a special need. I looked at my wife and said we have food and gas, so do you want to give what we have left? Remember, this is before credit cards and yes, people got their paychecks and stood in line at the bank to cash them. Then you put aside cash for your bills in envelopes. There is no fall back plan. She said yes. What happened was new to us. Both of us got major raises that week. We both worked hard. God's Word tells us that we can never out give him. He promises us that He will meet our needs, not all of our wants. His greatest blessings are way beyond temporal material things; He wants to transform us, free us and bless us right here right now.

## Chapter 6

# TRANSFORMATION

When Jesus told His disciples that He was leaving them they became more than just concerned. Jesus responds by letting them know that they are about to receive a new and wonderful promise.

- John 14:16-17: "And I will ask the Father, and **he will give you another advocate to help you and be with you forever—the Spirit of truth...**"

- John 14:26-27: "But the Advocate, **the Holy Spirit**, whom the Father will send in my name, **will teach you all things and will remind you of everything I have said to you.** Peace I leave with you; my peace I give you. I do not give to you as the world gives. Do not let your hearts be troubled and do not be afraid."

- John 16:7-13: "But very truly I tell you, ***it is for your good that I am going away. Unless I go away, the Advocate will not come to you;*** but if I go, I will send him to you. When he comes, he will prove the world to be in the wrong about sin and righteousness and judgment: about sin, because people do not believe in me; about righteousness, because I am going to the Father, where you can see me no longer; and about judgment, because the prince of this world now stands condemned. "I have much more to say to you, more than you can now bear. But when he, **the Spirit of truth, comes, he will guide you into all the truth.** He will not speak on his own; he will speak only what he hears, and ***he will tell you what is yet to come.***"

With God there is always more. Jesus reveals to them that He must go so that the Comforter (Holy Spirit/Advocate) can come. The Holy Spirit is the one who will guide the Disciples in writing the New Testament, which they do not yet realize.

The word Comforter ("paracletos" in the Greek) means: one called to the side of another for the purpose of helping that person. This means we will have within us the Holy Spirit, who will be our defender, helper and teacher during Christ's absence. Christ is now our Heavenly Advocate while the Holy Spirit is our Earthly Advocate. The Holy Spirit enters us when we repent and accept Christ as our Lord and Savior. It is His power that regenerates us and brings spiritual life to us. One of His tasks is to conform us to the image of Christ - to help us become more Christ-like, more loving! He is there to maintain a new and personal relationship with us. The Holy Spirit will start to sanctify us. He will use and apply the Word and bring conviction for our benefit.

Sanctification is the act or process of acquiring sanctity, of being made or becoming holy. To sanctify is to literally "set apart for particular use in a special purpose or work and to make holy or sacred."[4] The idea of positional sanctification is that at salvation we are completely forgiven. We are seen as holy, and have been sanctified in the sight of God, because of the work of Jesus Christ. When God looks at a person who has accepted Christ as his or her Savior, God sees a person completely perfect, holy, and justified as if he or she had never sinned. They are cloaked in Christ's righteousness! Practical, or progressive, sanctification is how we actually live day to day. The Bible states we start as babes in Christ (drinking milk) and move to Christian maturity (eating meat). Here are some verses speaking about the progressive nature of our Christian lives as it relates to sanctification:

- Galatians 2:20: "I have been crucified with Christ and I no longer live, **but Christ lives in me.** The life I now live in the body, I live by **faith in the Son of God**, who loved me and gave himself for me."

---

[4] https://en.wikipedia.org/wiki/Sanctification

Christ in me!

- Romans 12:1-2: "I beseech you therefore, brethren, by the mercies of God, that ye present your bodies a living sacrifice, holy, acceptable unto God, which is your reasonable service. And be not conformed to this world: but be ye **transformed by the renewing of your mind, that ye may prove what is that good, and acceptable, and perfect, will of God.**"

I presented myself. This is a life-long process and it can be a very painful process at times. I remember being newly saved. I thought that in five years I would be so together and mature in the Lord. As I heard the Word I committed myself to God. What I was not prepared for was the battle that would rage between my flesh and the Holy Spirit. I knew the Holy Spirit was given for my benefit. If I wanted to be transformed I must yield to His help. The Holy Spirit does not enter and take control. He is like God, a respecter of our free will. I must choose to cooperate.

I now understand what the Apostle Paul shared in:

- Romans 7:15-28: "I do not understand what I do. **For what I want to do I do not do, but what I hate I do.** And if I do what I do not want to do, I agree that the law is good. **As it is, it is no longer I myself who do it, but it is sin living in me.** For I know that good itself does not dwell in me, that is, in my sinful nature. **For I have the desire to do what is good, but I cannot carry it out.** For I do not do the good I want to do, **but the evil I do not want to do—this I keep on doing.** ......**What a wretched man I am!** Who will rescue me from this body that is subject to death? Thanks be to God, who delivers me through Jesus Christ our Lord..."

Today, with the Holy Spirit working in me forty plus years, I think back to my lack of understanding of how hard it is to change and do the right thing, even when you know what to do! In a small group I attend, we nicknamed it "***Slow Sanctifiers.***" Sad, but true. I resist God's agent of freedom - who only wants me free from the world's hold.

After about a year, the Holy Spirit started to help me see that I needed to deal with my hatred of my father. I would intellectually hear the Word of God and say Amen. Now, the Comforter was making me very uncomfortable. FORGIVE YOUR DAD! My Dad did not ask for my forgiveness, I replied. FORGIVE YOUR DAD! He doesn't deserve it. **FORGIVE YOUR DAD!** This went on for weeks until I finally yielded. As I wrote that letter of forgiveness, I told my Dad that I understood that, when he lost his father at eleven, he had no father figure to guide him. I understood that he had to work to support his family at the age of eleven. I understood that on December 8, 1941, he joined the Marines and saw the horror of war and the cruelty of man. I understood why he drank to forget the pain of seeing death all around him. I thanked him for having food on the table every day. Then I explained to him that God had placed me in his life and home for my benefit. Now that I understood this, I was able to forgive him for everything, and to have love in my heart for him because he had done his best. My Mom told me later how it impacted him. Truthfully, it impacted me a hundred times more. My hatred, my bitterness were gone. They were removed by God.

After about ten years of walking with Christ, God stopped me physically for a period of six weeks. I am a disabled veteran with a back injury that makes me unable to work when it flares up. I was completely immobilized. Five years prior to this incident, I started a business. When I began it, we had everything we needed. Suddenly, as the business grew, I wanted more and more. I even bought a new house without consulting my wife and surprised her (not smart). I now wanted a certain luxury car to show off my success (pride). The business meant less time for God and my family but it fed my ego. I knew Jesus' Word in:

- Matthew 6:24: "No one can serve two masters. Either you will hate the one and love the other, or you will be devoted to the one and despise the other. **You cannot serve both God and money.**"

Money is neutral - neither good nor bad. It comes down to how it affects you, and what are the costs to acquire it. During that six weeks I had time to stop and think. The Holy Spirit did provide guidance as promised and, with His wisdom, I made a decision. I shared with my wife that I felt we should close the business and sell everything and go back to how we lived before the business. She was thrilled. When I got my new job, I made a promise to her that I would not ever go into management and/or chase money or power. I was like an onion, peel back one layer and I discovered another layer that would need work.

Jesus says:

- <u>Matthew 5:8</u>: ***"Blessed are the pure in heart, for they will see God."***

- <u>Hebrews 12:14</u>: "Make every effort to live in peace with everyone and to be holy; ***without holiness no one will see the Lord.***"

<u>How can I have a pure heart?</u> I know my thoughts are not always pure.

- <u>Psalm 24:3-4</u>: "Who may ascend the mountain of the LORD? Who may stand in his holy place? ***The one who has clean hands and a pure heart***, who does not trust in an idol or swear by a false god."

Purity means single, not mixed. A pure heart is one that is void of all idols and has a single focus - Jesus. It is not about perfection. It is about your commitment, your focus, what occupies your thoughts, what or who holds your heart. I'm considered having a pure heart if Christ is the focus of my life. It is not some measurement of good deeds that I have done because I would fail every time.

King David was a man after God's heart. He showed his faith and commitment to the Lord. His faith was tested many times and he had many great successes, along with multiple failures. The Lord sent Nathan to King David with this rebuke,

- <u>2 Samuel 12:9-10</u>: "Why did you despise the word of the LORD by doing what is evil in his eyes? ***You struck down Uriah the Hittite with the sword and took his wife to be your own. You killed him with the sword of the Ammonites.*** Now, therefore, the sword will never depart from your house, because you despised me and took the wife of Uriah the Hittite to be your own."

David's response to his sin is:

- <u>Psalm 51:1-2</u>: "Have mercy on me, O God, according to your unfailing love; according to your great compassion blot out my transgressions. ***Wash away all my iniquity and cleanse me from my sin.***"

After his sin, David sought and received the Lord's forgiveness. David loved the Lord and His Law. David is a role model for all of us; a man after God's own heart; one who failed, sought and received God's mercy.

I remember when my best friend said something so true: "Everyone has to deal with sin. Each of us have a certain leaning or weakness that we will struggle with during our lives." Everything that I had been exposed to my first twenty-one years before I became saved, would need to be dealt with one by one with the help of the Holy Spirit. I would be a huge transformation project!

***Truth be told there are not a lot of big moments in our lives.*** Life is made up of thousands and thousands of little moments. We live in little moments. They are profoundly important. This is the key to living out the Christian life. I'm not proud of all my little moments in my marriage, in raising my children, in my secret thoughts, desires and wants.

Every day I must choose in those little moments what is right or wrong, whether I should go right or left, short term versus long term. My mind is able to do a complete analysis of my choices instantly. I know the short term benefit versus the long term consequence. I have a hard time choosing between short term and immediate gratification versus long term and saying "NO" to my desires. Even with the Holy Spirit, God's power in me, it is a struggle. I take two steps forward and one back. I have learned, after forty plus years as a Christian, that moving forward is the key. ***Perfection is not possible and, thanks be to God, it's not the requirement.*** Remember that "<u>**revival**</u>" is the work of the Holy Spirit. The Holy Spirit is the one who can stir a person or a whole nation to become authentic followers of Christ.

I do know that had I not had my first "Big Moment" in 1975, when I surrendered my will and accepted God's son Jesus as my Lord and Savior, it is highly likely that my life would have ended decades ago. You ask why would I think that? It is obvious to me what direction I would have chosen. If I had returned back to my old environment unchanged, I would have followed the same path to destruction that so many of my friends did. They died in their twenties, thirties and forties. **My course, my whole future, changed that one day in February 1975.**

One final thought about God's Love for those He has called, justified and will glorify one day. The Apostle Paul states:

- 2 Corinthians 12:6-10: "Even if I should choose to boast, I would not be a fool, because I would be speaking the truth. But I refrain, so no one will think more of me than is warranted by what I do or say, or because of these surpassingly great revelations. Therefore, in order **to keep me from becoming conceited, I was given a thorn in my flesh**, a messenger of Satan, to torment me. Three times I pleaded with the Lord to take it away from me. But he said to me, **"My grace is sufficient for you, for my power is made perfect in weakness."** Therefore I will boast all the more gladly about my weaknesses, so that Christ's power may rest on me. That is why, for Christ's sake, I delight in weaknesses, in insults, in hardships, in persecutions, in difficulties. For when I am weak, then I am strong."

The exact nature of Paul's thorn is purposefully left uncertain in Scripture. It is given in general terms so that whatever weakness, difficulty, hardship, burden, etc. that each of us receive is recognized as having a purpose. As part of God's Sovereign Will and His unlimited love for us, He gives each of us something that keeps us humble, and dependent on Him, out of His great love for us!

# Chapter 7

# DISCIPLESHIP

I became a disciple of the Lord Jesus Christ. What does that really mean? ***Disciple is someone who adheres to the teachings of another. I became a follower/learner/student of Jesus.***
Jesus was not educated to the standards of a Rabbi.

- John 7:15: "The Jews there were amazed and asked, 'How did this man [Jesus added] get such learning without having been taught?'"

Jesus did not select His disciples based on them first being tested on their knowledge of the Scriptures or other qualifications, like Rabbis. Jesus called who He wanted. His first five disciples: Peter, Andrew, James, John and Phillip were from Bethsaida, a small rural village in Israel with eight to ten family groups - no more than a few hundred people. Not one of these disciples would qualify for Rabbinical training. Why did Jesus call them? Was it because Jesus saw their hearts? ***They were the B Team according to this world.*** Why did Christ call me?

The first cost of discipleship I found in:

- Matthew 19:20-27: "'All these I have kept,' the young man said. 'What do I still lack?' Jesus answered, 'If you want to be perfect, go, sell your possessions and give to the poor, and you will have treasure in heaven. ***Then come, follow me.*** ' When the young man heard this, he went away sad, because he had great wealth. Then Jesus said to his disciples, 'Truly I tell you, ***it is hard for*** *someone who is rich to enter the kingdom of heaven.* Again I tell you, it is easier for a camel to go through the eye of a needle than for someone who is rich to enter the kingdom of God.' When the disciples heard this, they were greatly astonished and asked, 'Who then can be saved?' Jesus looked at them and said, 'With man this is impossible, **but with God all things are possible.**' Peter answered him**, 'We have left everything to follow you.'"**

I got the message of this passage. ***Jesus had to be first.***
Being a disciple begins with worship because that is what I owe Him for such a great salvation. Second, is obedience?

- John 14:21-24: "'Whoever has my commands and **keeps them is the one who loves me.** The one who loves me will be loved by my Father, and I too will love them and show myself to them.' Then Judas (not Judas Iscariot) said, 'But, Lord, why do you intend to show yourself to us and not to the world?' Jesus replied, 'Anyone who loves me will obey my teaching. My Father will love them, and we will come to them and make our home with them. *Anyone who does not love me will not obey my teaching.* These words you hear are not my own; they belong to the Father who sent me.'"

This meant that I was to read His word; not only read, but study and make it part of who I am. The third was found in:

- John 13:34-35: "A new command I give you: Love one another. As I have loved you, so you must love one another. *By this everyone will know that you are my disciples, if you love one another.*"

The fourth was found in:

- Matthew 28:18-20: "Then Jesus came to them and said, 'All authority in heaven and on earth has been given to me. *Therefore go and make disciples* of all nations, baptizing them in the name of the Father and of the Son and of the Holy Spirit, and teaching them to obey everything I have commanded you. And surely I am with you always, to the very end of the age.'"

Disciple means Witnessing!

## Discipleship Is Not Easy, but Worth It!

Salvation is free, but discipleship will always cost something. This is a calling where Jesus wants us to use our different gifts, different talents and abilities for the benefit of His church.

- Luke 9:23-25: "Then he said to them all: *'Whoever wants to be my disciple must deny themselves and take up their cross daily and follow me. For whoever wants to save their life will lose it, but whoever loses their life for me will save it. What good is it for someone to gain the whole world, and yet lose or forfeit their very self?'"*

I really had no idea of the cost that would be involved. I also had no idea as to the blessings that would be received. Basically, as a new believer, I was just beginning my walk as a disciple, and was truly clueless!

- Acts 1:8: "But you will *receive power when the Holy Spirit comes on you*; and you will be *my witnesses* in Jerusalem, and in all Judea and Samaria, and to the ends of the earth."

Jesus promised the Holy Spirit would come and we would receive power to enable us to be able and bold in witnessing. We are empowered by the Holy Spirit in us.

- Mark 13:11: "Whenever you are arrested and brought to trial, do not worry beforehand about what to say. *Just say whatever is given you at the time, for it is not you speaking, but the Holy Spirit.*"

Scripture tells us not to worry about what to say because the Holy Spirit will provide us with the words. The Holy Spirit knows exactly what needs to be said. This helped me with my fear of witnessing. All I needed to learn was to be instantly obedient and do/say what the Holy Spirit wanted me to do or say. How would I know if it was the Holy Spirit? It could be one of three possibilities. First, it could just be me talking to myself. Second, it could be Satan. Third, it might be the Holy Spirit. The first time the Holy Spirit prompted me to witness to someone, my mind had a quick internal discussion/debate. I had to decide if the small still voice prompting me was really the Holy Spirit. I knew Satan did not want me witnessing about Christ. I knew it was not me because that thought was not something I would come up with on my own. By elimination, it had to be the Holy Spirit.

I'm at work. I have never called my older brother during the day. The Holy Spirit tells me to call him because my brother was in trouble. I immediately called his home number just as he was walking into his house. When my brother picked up the phone I said to him: "God just told me to call you. Why are you in trouble?" My brother was, to say the least, quite taken aback. He <u>was</u> in trouble and what had happened was less than thirty minutes earlier.

It is Monday morning and I had just arrived at work. The Holy Spirit tells me to call a friend on his cell phone. I immediately call my friend's cell phone. When he answers, I find out that he had a heart attack during the weekend. They were preparing him for heart surgery. I prayed with him. When I later saw him, he said he had been so scared, but after the prayer he felt God's peace come upon him.

When we understand that all we need to do is our small part by being obedient, God does the rest. He does the heavy lifting. God will empower, guide, and provide everything we need to be His disciples and do whatever ministries He chooses. He does this by prompting us and then opening the doors to service in His name, while empowering us by His Holy Spirit.

It is 1977, and the Lord provided our initial ministry. We were team teachers for the High School Sunday School class. Later, it would include the college-aged students as well. The cost was the amount of time it took to read, study and prepare lessons. The blessing was being involved with young people who would accept, and grow in, Christ. We have so many memories. Some great, some good and some heart breaking.

We would always get the question from our students "Is it ok to date an unsaved person?" I stated, "Certainly. First date is the interview to get as much information as you can. The second date is then Sunday school, church or youth group." One morning, a young man brought his date from the previous evening to our Sunday school class. I noticed she had her arms crossed. He introduced her and she immediately said she was told that I could explain Creation/Evolution differences. I said I could and asked her if she had twenty-six weeks. She stayed, accepted Christ, and eventually married that young man. This young man became a pastor for Christ. We would have our students for six years. We had such fun hosting summer barbeques, trips to the beach, and gatherings for our annual Christmas party.

One of the most tragic incidents that tested our Spiritual understanding was going to be the life of one of our Sunday school students. She had just completed her first year at a Christian college when I received a call to go see her at the hospital. She had just been dealt a terrible blow. She was diagnosed with leukemia. She immediately said her life was over. I shared with her that all we knew was that she had leukemia and the direction of her life had taken a new turn. As we spoke, we talked about what had not changed: God is Sovereign, His love for her was the same, and she had His call on her life. Her life became one of sheer testimony for the goodness of God. Sometime after her diagnosis, her mother called us and said she was coming to our house for the annual Sunday school Christmas party. Her mother's words to us were, "make sure she has a good time." We did not have to make sure she had a good time; she always brought that with her. One week later she was taken from us and now resides in heaven. My wife was one of those who was honored to speak at the memorial service. My wife shared this sweet girl's greatest desire was to see all of us in heaven and that no one would be left behind. Many of her family members have since made the decision to see her in heaven, too.

As I shared previously, my father bought everything from the underground economy, and most of it was stolen. It was early 1978, when my father asked me if I wanted a brand new color console. I told him "No." I added it was stealing to buy stolen merchandise. As a new Christian, I actually said, "If God wants me to have a color console then he will give it to me." That was opening my mouth and inserting my foot, a.k.a. new, immature believer. My father immediately jumped on it with, "Your God can't!" When my father came over to our new home for the first time a few months later, he saw a color console in my family room. He asked me, "Did God give that to you, son?" Well, as a matter of fact, God did and

*I Am, Therefore I Know*

this is how: the Christian businessman man for whom I worked told me to buy any color television I wanted and send him the bill. This man had no idea that I had previously put my foot in my mouth. I told my Dad the story and handed him the receipt. I have seen God's Hand work like this all my life. God was teaching me, a new believer, that He is the "I AM."

God also has a real sense of humor. After Sunday service we would stop by and see my parents. This particular Sunday, my Dad was fit to be tied. So I ventured to ask him what was upsetting him so much. He told me that someone had stolen their patio set off the porch the day before. I responded with, "Dad I knew that patio set I bought last night for $100 bucks looked familiar." He replied, "That's not funny." I said, "Really?" At this point, he did break into a full grin and laugh! I have been asked by different folks if I believe I will see my father in heaven? I have always answered it this way *"If someone can tell me the limits of grace then I could know."* I do not know the heart of any other individual but my own. Only God does!

In August of 1979, my wife and I decided that I would return full time to college and finish my Engineering degree. We thought it was a wise decision and had prayed it through. We had been married at this point just over three years and we wanted this out of the way before having our first child. Our first daughter was born June 1980, which meant she was conceived about a week after I started college. That meant putting my college education on hold. We were learning to trust God even when he **closes** a door and we have to change course. I did finish my Engineering degree at night by 1987, before my father passed away in 1991. We had a son in October 1982, and our youngest daughter in August 1984.

We were praying for a solution to be able to afford Christian school for our children when God **opened** the door for my wife to work at the Christian school for a small salary in 1987. However, the two major benefits were free tuition for our three children and her being off when they were off, including summers. God had solved what we thought was impossible - how to add income, pay for Christian school and make it possible for my wife to be with the children.

- Romans 12:9-18: *"Love must be sincere.* Hate what is evil; cling to what is good. Be devoted to one another in love. Honor one another above yourselves. ***Never be lacking in zeal, but keep your spiritual fervor,*** serving the Lord. Be joyful in hope, patient in affliction, and faithful in prayer. Share with the Lord's people who are in need. Practice hospitality. ***Bless those who persecute you; bless and do not curse.*** Rejoice with those who rejoice; mourn with those who mourn. ***Live in harmony with one another.*** Do not be proud, <u>**but be willing to associate with people of low position.**</u> Do not be conceited. Do not repay anyone evil for evil. Be careful to do what is right in the eyes of everyone."

Living in harmony and being willing to associate with people of low position would be tested.

It is 1987, and I had been a disciple for about twelve years - attending church in this denomination for ten years. I was nominated and voted onto our church's board. The pastor of this church was my spiritual father and my mentor. Our Board consisted of three deacons, nine trustees and the pastor. I am the guy who enters the room all smiles, who wants to enjoy all the moments of life. Special occasions are to be celebrated and I usually overdid it. Life at this moment was good. I got elected to the board because I had matured enough - at least from the outside. The heart still had an invisible sign that God could see, saying ***"Work Needed."*** I was soon to find out why you do not want to put new Christians on Boards. Being six foot two, 220 pounds and somewhat athletic would be a major plus at my second board meeting. The meeting started off in prayer and went south quickly. What I did not know was this was typical. A few of my brothers in Christ started disrespecting one another with elevated voices. These were our church's most senior and mature brethren. I sat directly across from my pastor and mentor. I was just a junior member, brand new and had served many years less in the Lord than those around me. After about fifteen minutes, I could take it no more. I stood up and looked at the four men who were out of order. I calmly stated in a level voice that, as of today, this kind of behavior would stop. All would respect and honor their brothers, or one or all four of them were going out to the parking lot to settle the dispute right now. I saw a twinkle in my pastor's eye, four other trustees looking at me with hope and one trustee who stood up and said "he can take all four of you and I'm ready to see it." This was never

*I Am, Therefore I Know*

repeated. What was interesting was that if I voted with one group against the other opposing group, they would come to me later and say, "Glad you stood with us," to which my reply was always, "I felt you had the correct position." I am certain any of you who have served on boards or juries have plenty of stories to tell.

That same year, after completing my Engineering degree, I was prompted to start an inner city basketball ministry. We met Tuesday and Thursday evenings from 6:30 to 9:00, which included about 25-30 minutes for a talk and prayer. After the first three weeks, I realized that having the sharing about Jesus at the end, followed by prayer, was not working. At the end of basketball, they slipped away. I moved it to the middle and they all stayed and listened. These were men from the streets and they were a little rough around the edges. I had three rules. No foul language, if you cursed it was considered a turnover - amazing how quickly they were able to control their mouths. Second, no fighting - one punch and you were barred from coming back. Three, calls/fouls were to be respected. It would take about two years for a person to become receptive to the messages and the prayers. They wanted to play so they all stuck around.

I found out that this type of ministry put one on the front lines. Suddenly, you are dealing with people who have all kinds of situations that need solutions. One night, one of the guys who had been coming for about two years, came in and, as soon as I saw him, I knew that something was seriously wrong. I stopped play and walked over and asked him what was going on. He had come from the hospital where, earlier that day, his daughter had been born with a hole in her heart. He did not have medical insurance. Most of the men who came were in the same position. It was hard to see this man full of fear and with tears in his eyes, not sure what his new daughter's future held. Everyone surrounded him and laid hands on him as we prayed for God to provide a miracle. The following week he was back with a bunch of his buddies. He shared that, when the doctor double-checked his daughter before surgery, they discovered the hole was gone, repaired, healed. The man today is a pastor of a Hispanic church. That winter we had the most men ever come to Christ in a single season.

It is 1990, and I am at a board meeting. On the agenda that night is the Basketball Ministry. One of the deacons made a motion that the basketball ministry really did not fit the church's vision and should be closed down. It really was about race, class, **_people of low position_**, economic differences, etc. The players made some people uncomfortable because they were different. You have to realize that some of these men had spent time in prison. Since I was in charge of that ministry, I was asked to speak to the motion. I shared that we had never had any incidents and foul language was never a problem. Then I added that if you reject them you are rejecting me and I will resign and leave the church. The response was, "Brother, we love you and want you to stay!" I reminded them not to be fooled by the suit, the car and the fact that I spoke Christianese. I was, and will always be, one of them **_(people of low position)_**. The only difference is I have been redeemed by Christ and it is our church's job and mission to give each person that same chance. Who are we to decide their fate? We voted. The man who would take over the basketball ministry when I retired at the age of forty-seven had gone to prison before he met Christ through basketball. He then went on to meet his Christian wife in the church. At his wedding, his five groomsmen were from the basketball ministry. I got a tap on my shoulder from that deacon, and friend, who said we voted right that night and God gets the glory for the work that had been done in these men's lives.

There is another ministry where you get to see miracles. As a Deacon we visit those in the hospitals and many times only a miracle of God provides a person a second chance. I got a call from the church secretary to go to Taylor Hospital. When I arrived, there sat a young man waiting for me. His family was assembled in a private room. He shared that his sister had overdosed on drugs and they were told that her vitals were dropping. He shared that none of his family had much spiritual understanding. As I entered the room, there were six to seven family members. I apologized for having to meet them under such circumstances. They seemed glad. I asked them if they would mind if we prayed for her, at which point they informed me that someone else had prayed for her. They explained a priest had prayed and departed. I carefully shared with them that God is in control and that He is able to help. However, He (God) is not obligated to help or solve this situation for us. (The truth was their daughter had placed herself in this desperate and life-ending position.) We all bowed our heads and I prayed. We prayed that God would be **_merciful_** to us who do not deserve His blessings. In about thirty seconds, the door flung open and the nurse said she did not know what had happened but all of her vitals changed and she was rapidly improving. The family hoped that this merciful intervention would have caused their daughter to change the course of her life. She, however, went on to jail. God, why did you raise up this young lady on drugs? Yet, this is the privy of God! He is the "I AM" and He gives us more chances to **PERHAPS** choose Him than we know.

Being a disciple and being involved in ministry, as well as serving on boards, was eye opening. Some days were great and other days not so good. When you take a moment and consider Who it is Who calls us, then it is all good and we get the honor of being in His service. We are His ambassadors!

In 1987, we had the opportunity to attend a marriage weekend. God again had opened another door of service. The following year, we were one of two sharing couples who would share their lives and marriage during these weekend marriage retreats. This was a gift from God, because twice a year we received incredible marriage building teachings from Christian authors and speakers. Ministry again gave us back so much more than what we put in. God knew our marriage needed lots of help. We nicknamed our first year of marriage "Star Wars." That about says it all.

I started a new position in February 1986, in what would be my final career and company. I would work there until December of 2016, at one of the largest companies in America. Our division was considered small at six thousand employees. Being an aerospace company, I was told that I would be lucky to last more than a few years, since that business has employment cycles with severe ups and downs. I remember my first eight years there we had multiple layoffs.

- 1 Peter 4:14: "If you *are insulted because of the name of Christ*, you are blessed, for the Spirit of glory and of God rests on you."

I knew that some folks made fun of my walk with Christ behind my back. They even put Reverend in front of my name. It was okay. I just worked hard and earned another nickname "Rocket Man." It, too, was okay because I did my part to stay off the layoff list and trusted God to do the rest.

I do not know how God does what only He can do! Here is what transpired over a six year period. It began back in 1988, in the Aircraft Developmental and Test Building. There was a new second level supervisor assigned over us. He had about fifty aircraft support personnel, I being one of them.

- <u>Acts 5:27-29</u>: "The apostles were brought in and made to appear before the Sanhedrin to be questioned by the high priest. 'We gave you strict orders not to teach in this name,' he said. 'Yet you have filled Jerusalem with your teaching and are determined to make us guilty of this man's blood.' Peter and the other apostles replied: **'We must obey God rather than human beings!'"**

When this new supervisor arrived, the non-management bully of our organization gave each of us **strict orders not to teach (or help) him and that we should do our best to undermine him.** After six months, the bully found out that I was helping and teaching our new second level boss the ropes. It was about two in the afternoon. I was at my desk when I heard my name screamed, and I was called to come immediately. When I stood in front of the bully's desk, he asked me if I was helping this new supervisor. I said "yes" in a very easy and non-raised voice. He asked, "What do you not understand about not helping him?" Now picture this: there are over 200 people quietly listening on this open floor and there are about twenty managers at their office doors watching intently to see where this is going. Not one of them moved to help. I answered him again in a calm steady voice "I do not work for you the last time I checked." He lost it and then threatened to meet me outside and beat me to a pulp. His words were more colorful! I looked at him and asked him to carefully consider what I was about to say. I told him that I was street hardened by fighting all the time as a youth, I was military trained, I took martial arts and I was ten years younger, six inches taller, with forty pounds more muscle and had an arm length of thirty-five inches. I said I would be more than glad to meet him anywhere, anytime. At which point he screamed at me to leave, which I did. As I returned to my desk the Manager of the whole building signaled for me to come to his office. When I walked in, I looked back and saw 15-20 other managers behind me. I was asked to press charges since I was threatened by this bully. I said, "I never felt threatened. You created

*I Am, Therefore I Know*

him. He is your problem." Obviously, the new supervisor heard all about it. As a result, I made a life-long friend just by obeying the Word of God and doing the right thing! **My friend** was later promoted and transferred to the Seattle division.

It is now 1994, and I am requested to change product lines to help one that is in trouble. When I arrive, there is a decision to have a major layoff. I find out that this new management team is not going to protect me. I go to the top guy of our organization, who was retiring August 31, 1994. I ask for his help and he said, "It's the next guy's call." The problem was that, if I was back on my previous product line, I would be secure. Because they (this product line) requested my help, I'm now at risk. It is Friday lunch, about two and half weeks before the September 1st lay-off. I am finishing my lunch at my desk when **my friend** had just returned back from the Seattle division. We talked for over an hour and I brought him up to speed on what had changed while he was away. Then he asked, "How are you?" I told him what was going on. He told me he was the new big boss and would take care of it. The next day, when his 30 plus managers arrived in the totem trailers where they ranked employees, he walked over to my name on the wall and put a star on it and said, "This man is untouchable. Do you understand?" When my two new product line managers returned, they came up to me and asked how I knew him. All I said was, "We are tight and one word from me and you are both gone." Both later became good friends, especially after I fixed their broken processes. The Sovereignty of God's Will and His care for us never ceases to amaze me.

- Matthew 10:28-31: "Do not be afraid of those who kill the body but cannot kill the soul. Rather, be afraid of the One who can destroy both soul and body in hell. Are not two sparrows sold for a penny? Yet not one of them will fall to the ground outside your Father's care. ***And even the very hairs of your head are all numbered. So don't be afraid;*** you are worth more than many sparrows."

What knowledge, what power to be able to arrange this and millions of other circumstances so they conform to His Will and for our benefit.

- <u>1 Peter 5:7</u>: "***Cast all your anxiety on him because he cares for you.***"

I was extremely anxious waiting for God's help! Will I ever know how much He cares? Hopefully, one day.

Here is another example of the benefit of serving God. When my company provided us unrestricted internet at work I knew that this new temptation had some downsides. One day I received, along with over a hundred other individuals, an email loaded with pornographic material. I immediately hit reply all and requested that my name be removed and that if I received another I would call security and report the sender. I was removed. Two months later, people who were engaging in this activity were reprimanded. Punishment varied from time off to loss of their jobs, which ended many careers.

- <u>Matthew 5: 11</u>: "Blessed are you when people insult you, **persecute you and falsely say all kinds of evil against you because of me.**"

As a Christian author, I would not sell either of my books to fellow employees at my place of employment. There were many friends who wanted signed copies as gifts, as well as books for family and friends. They would give them to their family and friends hoping they would read it and PERHAPS consider Christ. Most of the books I handed out at work were for one purpose: PERHAPS! About three years before I retired, someone put in a formal complaint that I was writing my third book on company time. I believe he/she got the idea when an executive was fired for doing just that. The investigation I was told took over two months. Once the complaint came in, they immediately pulled down every type of digital evidence available. This meant for the previous four weeks, when the complaint was submitted, they looked at every key stroke I typed on my computer for the whole month. They reviewed my Outlook meeting schedules and where I was for the month by the tracking data kept by the chip in my access/security badge. They even checked the computer that I used in the classified area when doing secret work. Finally, I got called in and they explained what I had been accused of and how the process worked. I was asked if I wanted representation which I said was not needed.

The investigator provided his background and qualifications which were quite impressive. First, he stated he had not ever investigated someone that everyone who was queried said it was not possible for the person to do what he was accused. He said my entire management team said, "No way!" If I was found guilty, I would be fired and lose my pension. I was asked if I was writing my third book. I answered, "No." He said, "I know. We even checked with your publisher. I'm going to be writing the report this week. It will state that you were targeted because of your Christian beliefs and witness. It will also state that there were **only seventeen minutes** of time that could not be accounted for in the entire month."

In June of 2000, my wife resigned her position after fourteen years in the Christian school our children had attended. She was looking forward to working for a new company started by a close friend and dear brother in Christ. In the first week of July, she found out that his partner had jeopardized the company's solvency. We watched a promising prospect and salary vaporize. For us it was a salaried position, but for our brother in Christ it was his life's work. Week two of July in that same summer, I went in for my annual physical. The next day I found myself in the hospital being tested. If you return home from the hospital and your doctor calls you within fifteen minutes of the completion of the tests, that's not good. ***Three days later I had surgery for cancer of the colon. I was only forty-seven at the time.*** There was no history of cancer anywhere in my family, my wife needed me, and my kids were shocked. What shocked them most was that Dad was "broken." The fact that I was human and not always going to be there with them was a new revelation. The results of the biopsy were sent off to two different pathological teams for review. Anyone who has been told that they have cancer runs the full gamut of possibilities inside their heads while they await the results determining their fate. Did people pray for me? Yes thankfully. People asked how I was handling it. Was I prepared? I understood that Christ had removed the sting of death. I really had no fear of death. Like most people, I preferred not to take the express train to heaven. I wanted to live a long life like everyone else. I wanted to be here for my wife and my children and my future grandchildren.

However, I knew the Truth that sets one free. I knew God was for me. I knew He (God) is Sovereign. I knew if my ministry on earth was done for Him (Jesus), then His Word declared that no harm would befall me (this does not mean absence of problems or testing). I also knew that if He (God) decided it was time to go home to heaven, then I would have no say in it. This brought me peace, and I rested in this knowledge and truth. However, my wife and kids were not in the same state. Truth be told, those left behind deal with the tragedy of the loss of loved ones. I shared that if it was reversed, and my wife had the cancer, then I would have been exactly the same as my wife was about me. God sent a message to me. Everyone prayed for healing, but God did not send that message.

The men of the church had previously scheduled a men's retreat down at the shore. The speaker that day rose to speak, not knowing about my cancer. He stopped, then said the Lord had given him something to share for someone who was there that day. He went on to share before he started his teaching:

> **"They had unearthed a Roman coin from the fourth century and on it was an ox. The ox had one eye on the plough and the other eye on 'the altar of sacrifice. There was an inscription on the bottom of the coin that, when translated, said 'PREPARED FOR EITHER.'"**

God did not tell me that I was healed. What He did tell me was that His ways are higher than our ways and that He (God) gave me an eloquent way to share His wonderful truth. His providence decided that I would get to stay behind the plough in His service for a little while longer.

- <u>Psalm 91:11-12</u>: *"The LORD will command his angels to take good care of you. They will lift you up in their hands. Then you won't trip over a stone."*

My youngest daughter was driving home one Friday night in a driving rain. As she slowed down to take a curve on a country road, her car left the road. She traveled approximately ten feet, at which time she collided with a solid stone wall with full dirt reinforcement behind it. She then careened back across two lanes of traffic, finally resting on the opposite grassy shoulder, easily fifty feet or more from the initial impact site. We got the call no parent wants. After arriving, I surveyed the damage to the car. She described what happened in detail. As I looked over the scene, the car, and the wall, I asked my daughter - who was not injured - to please review again each detail with me. We looked at the wall and observed that it had been hit with enough force to destroy the wall and should have created a sizable amount of damage to the car. Miraculously, the headlights, the bumper, and the quarter panels were not damaged. They had scratches to be painted later. The air bags were still intact. I walked my daughter over to the wall. She looked over all the evidence and events and summarized it as well as anyone could. She said an angel must have taken the brunt of the force between her and the wall. She had two blown tires and the front axle cross bars snapped. Why some damage if there was an intervention? Maybe there was a message God wanted to make sure was received. We cannot say for certain. That night was the first time my wife and I shared with our daughter an incident of divine intervention involving the both of us: we were new believers; it was early 1978, and we were driving behind a truck carrying a load of steel plates. Suddenly, a steel plate came off the back of the truck. There was no time; it was going to come through our windshield with the potential to sever us in two. There was a tremendous bang! The steel plate went over the car and landed on the road. I pulled off the road. As I got out of the car, I began to circle it looking for damage. I got back in the car and asked my wife, "Did you hear that bang and see the plate?" She said, "Yes." I told her there was no damage. God's angels spared us. The question is how many other times has God and His mighty army of angels protected us and we were unaware?

At a Thanksgiving dinner with all of our now adult children home, the subject of car accidents was brought up. My son's two sisters were teasing their brother about his four car accidents in his first two years of driving. His first response was that only one counted. A chorus of whys was heard. "Three were minor and only the one that the police came counts." Then he added, "Anyway, it's not my fault." His sisters, knowing him, couldn't wait for this one. My son stated it was Dad's fault because all the Mills' Angels are always protecting Dad and his car! We all died laughing.

The marriage ministry that we have been involved with for almost thirty years has a store that was previously a Kiddie City toy store. At the end of our marriage weekends, the whole team meets for dinner after the participants leave. We were now the host couple for the weekends and I am on the Board. One Sunday, the Holy Spirit moved me to share about my sordid past with the team. This night I shared some of my past *(person of low position)*, such as robbing this Kiddie City when I was young, and about God's sense of humor. To think He would call a street kid who had robbed Kiddie City regularly, and now it is one of the sites that supports a ministry that I love. We all had a good chuckle.

I have shared at multiple Homeless Shelters in our area. I remember the first time I went to City Center in Chester. The woman introduced me as a successful member of the church and a Christian author of two books. I removed the podium and I pulled up a stool and sat down. Then I said to them "Hi, I'm JUST and my first name." They responded with "Hi, JUST and my first name." I was there as an equal and they knew it. I began to share about my background and how I became homeless. None of these people had to come and listen. They could save thirty minutes and just come for food. When I was finished speaking, a man stood up and said he knew me from 'back in the day.' He said it was all true and he was not allowed to associate with me. He was raised as a Christian and, because of drugs, he lost everything - including his wife and children. We spoke afterwards and I reminded him, "God is the God of second chances, call to Him and He will help."

Presently, my wife and I are in two small groups at our church. In one small group is the under-cover officer who was assigned to my street in order to stop the drug trade and crime spree forty years ago. God does have a sense of humor! When I chose to follow Jesus, I put in motion more than I will ever understand. The love, the care, the protection, the opportunity - whether educationally, at work, or in ministry, our day-to-day provision, our future inheritance, our new glorified body are all a result of His great love for us. Yes, there is a cost. My wife and I volunteered to teach; we learned the Word of God as a result. When my wife and I volunteered to be involved in a marriage ministry our relationship grew and our marriage benefitted. When I started the basketball ministry my belief in miracles grew the same as those folks who had nothing to depend on but miracles from God. God also provided mentors, the gifts, and the power necessary to live for Him. Over time, the Holy Spirit has been slowly developing in me the Fruit of the Spirit.

- <u>Galatian 5:22-23</u>: "But the fruit of the Spirit is love, joy, peace, forbearance, kindness, goodness, faithfulness, gentleness and self-control. Against such things there is no law."

All through my life God has been there! Each change of job, each move to a different home, and the timing of events in our lives are ordered by God down to the smallest detail. No one could have arranged and/or planned all of my life's events with such care and love like this, except the "I AM!

## Chapter 8

# DIFFERENCES

There are a variety of denominations. How do we choose? Who has the truth? Let me provide a baseline for those who, like me, may have had no religious foundation.

Orthodox Christianity is the starting point. "Orthodox" comes from two Greek words that stand for "Right Belief" or "Right Opinion." By the 2nd Century, Christians saw the need for separating right Christian beliefs from various kinds of subtle heresies. Webster defines "heresy" as "an opinion held in opposition to the commonly received doctrine and tending to promote division and dissension." The plumb line of measuring Christianity to other faiths is found in:

- <u>1 Corinthians 15:3-4:</u> *"For what I received I passed on to you as of first importance: that Christ died for our sins according to the Scriptures, that he was buried, that he was raised on the third day according to the Scriptures"*

*This is of FIRST IMPORTANCE. Christ died for our sins!* Why Christ? He was the sinless sacrifice. *We are sinners.* Our nature is to rebel and to sin, or disobey, God. *What Christ did was according to the Scriptures;* Christ came and fulfilled the Scriptures perfectly. *Christ was buried and rose again on the third day;* Christ paid for sin, which means salvation is available only one way – through Christ. What does that mean?

- <u>Ephesians 2:8-9</u>: "For it is by grace you have been saved, through faith and this not from yourselves, it is the gift of God not by works, so that no one can boast."

This is the fundamental basis of comparison. False churches add other requirements for salvation, such as "works." Christian creeds are universal statements about God and what He has revealed to His church. All true Christian Churches would have these as part of their foundational core beliefs. Three simple examples:

<u>The Bible is verbally inspired of God</u>, not just ideas but even the choice of words. The original writers were moved by God to write what He wanted them to say.

<u>God is, and has always been</u>. He is the Creator of the heavens and earth. He is the One who redeems and saves man from sin. God has revealed himself as a single Being consisting of three interrelated persons: the Father, Son, and Holy Spirit. Some refer to this as the Trinity, others as a Triunity. To tell you the truth, no one fully understands how it works – how one Being can be God, Jesus, and the Holy Spirit doing three different roles. God is on His throne as Father. God is Jesus the Son and is sitting at His own right side. The Holy Spirit lives inside the believer. How does one Being do all this? This remains a mystery.

<u>Salvation is deliverance from spiritual death and the enslavement of sin</u>. Salvation is freely provided by God through the Blood of Christ. Salvation is received by a person when:

1) One repents before God for sins and sinful nature, or inclinations.
2) One believes or has faith in the fact that the death and resurrection of Jesus Christ removes and brings forgiveness for sin.
3) In response to placing faith in God's love, one experiences the regeneration (rebirth), the renewing work of the Holy Spirit, and is declared righteous (right with God).

At the moment of salvation, a person becomes part of God's family. God is the father now, and one becomes joint heirs with Christ, having the promised hope of eternal life from God Himself. These revealed truths are the foundation of what separates Christianity from all false religions.

Jesus prayed that we would have unity. Why are there many different denominations, giving the impression that Christianity is fractured? The review of history shows the early church as unified and loosely organized. Once the church becomes the Roman Empire's official religion, a mixing of Christianity with paganism begins. Eventually, the Bishop of Rome declares himself head over all the bishops. This causes the Church to divide between East and West. As we follow history, we find that the ***Church that is centered in Rome was a false church.*** The true church is forced to go underground, just like the early church did under the Roman Empire. The Eastern Orthodox Church falls and their scholars are scattered across Europe. Finally, the reformation happens in Europe and the true church reappears. However, history and circumstance have combined for some unique changes.

We have to go back 400 years to the century following the Protestant Reformation. If your King was Catholic you had better be Catholic. If he suddenly changed to Protestantism then you changed, too. Even worse is they went to war over it. Non-conformity could not be tolerated and religion was worth fighting for. They fought each other to a point of sheer exhaustion and, at the end of this religiously motivated Thirty Years War, called a truce. When the Peace of Westphalia was signed in 1648, ***it allowed Calvinism to join Lutheranism and Catholicism as recognized expressions of the Christian faith.*** This stopped the war but it laid the foundation of what was to be known as territorial religion. You could believe what you wanted, but you had to move to the territory with the same beliefs. Anabaptists, who were non-territorial, were persecuted because they lived in the wrong territories.

## DENOMINATIONAL THEORY

England, in 1529 was the first country to break from the Roman Catholic Church, was having problems among the different Protestant groups. The Presbyterians, who held the majority vote at the Westminster Assembly in 1642-49, developed what would later be known as the ***Denominational Theory.*** The minority vote at the Westminster Assembly was the Congregationalists. These two groups, the Presbyterians and Congregationalists, were successful at understanding how to have

Christian unity even in disagreement. This Denominational Theory was based on the following principles.

**First**, recognizing the human inability to always see the truth clearly, differences of opinion about the outward form of the church are inevitable. **We tend to see things differently from each other.**

**Second**, these principles apply as long as the differences do not involve FUNDAMENTALS OF FAITH. An example on a non-fundamental would be Baptism of Water: some dunk, some sprinkle.

**Third**, since no church has a final and full grasp of the Divine truth, the true church of Christ can never be represented by any single ecclesiastical structure. The truth is no church is without error. *It is not if we err, it is the degree of error.* All man-made doctrines based on human interpretation of the Scriptures, are going to be in error to some degree. All human writing will have some kind of error present. This writing is not error-proof because it is made with human hands and I know it and accept that fact.

**Fourth**, separation does not constitute schism. Does one have to agree with every detail of their denomination's doctrines? No. Scripture is the only revealed and inspired Word of God. *All other documents are subject to Scripture.*

In the New World (America), being "denominated" meant any group claiming the authority of Christ and truth based on the Bible was separate and, at the same time, one member of a larger group known as "The Church." The Apostle Paul said of those who differed with him, "Christ is preached and in this I rejoice." *Unity is found in Christ only.* I am with Christians from different denominations regularly and yet I have experienced unity and oneness of spirit and attitude with them.

*The religious freedom I have today to worship God the way I see fit is a blessing of Denominationalism.* It is the best plan for humans who are imperfect and have sinful natures. Yes, it would be better to have one universal Christian church with no division to present to this world. However, as soon as you add men into it, the possibilities of abuse are so overwhelming that I believe all religious freedom would be lost. This book would not be allowed; only sanctioned material coming from official sources would be distributed. America is a Republic with an extremely inefficient form of government. A dictatorship is a much more efficient decision-making government. There is only one problem. Where do you find dictators who can be trusted? America has its inefficient government because our founding fathers had a clear Biblical understanding of human nature; thus, all the checks and balances with the division of powers. ***The church may appear to be fractured, but in reality it is in its safest form.***

## OUR COMBINED HISTORY

In Acts, the Scriptures share the beginning of the Church. There was nothing but resistance to the spread of the Gospel. Once a church was established, false teachings and the sins of the church would need to be addressed. Paul writes in **49 A.D.** to the Galatians:

- Galatians 3:1-5: "You foolish Galatians! Who has bewitched you? Before your very eyes Jesus Christ was clearly portrayed as crucified. I would like to learn just one thing from you: Did you receive the Spirit by observing the law, or ***by believing*** what you heard? Are you so foolish? After beginning with the Spirit, are you now trying to attain your goal by ***human effort?*** Have you suffered so much for nothing - if it really was for nothing? Does God give you his Spirit and work miracles among you because you observe the law, or because you believe what you heard?"

The Galatians started off by faith in Christ, then the Christian Jews were adding the keeping of the Law back on top of the grace and freedom of God. It does not take long for believers to get off track and depend upon works and return back to sin.

All of the Apostles were martyred except John, who died in exile on the isle of Patmos. The task of completing the New Testament was now complete **(95 A.D.)**.

Christianity would spread throughout the Empire against unbelievable resistance in spite of the power of Rome. Then in the 4th Century things would change dramatically.

Constantine, who was a young officer in Rome, escaped from his watchers and rode night and day until joining his father Constantius in the British campaign. The Gallic army, deeply loyal to the humane Constantius, felt the same about Constantine. So, when his father died at

*I Am, Therefore I Know*

York, they recognized him as Caesar and Augustus – Emperor in 306 A.D. Galerius, too distant to affect this turn of events, reluctantly recognized him as a Caesar. Constantine and his father never followed the rest of the empire in the persecution of the Christians. Resultant, his armies had many Christians and he saw their immediate and long-term value to the empire by bringing their high level of ethics, which was something Rome had lost. By 307, there were six Caesars and one Emperor, Calerius; who died in 311. Constantine's conversion was either an act of religious belief or a stroke of political genius. Helena, his mother, became a Christian and is said to have acquainted her son with the truth of the invisible God.

**On October 27, 312**, Constantine met the forces of Maxentius at Saxa Rubra (Red Rocks) nine miles north of Rome. On the afternoon prior to the battle, Constantine saw a flaming cross in the sky, with the Greek words "en toutoi nika" – "in this sign conquer." His soldiers were supposedly told to put a cross upon their shields. Maxentius makes a critical error in strategy and was caught with his back against the Tiber with no retreat possible except over the Mulvian Bridge. Constantine forces secured the bridge and Maxentius perished in the Tiber along with thousands of his troops.

**Early in 313**, Constantine and Licinius met in Milan to work out their rule. Constantine and Licinius issued the "Edict of Milan." This ordered the return of Christians' property and rights.

**In 326 A.D.** the incredible elevation of **Christianity as the empire's official religion would happen.** The world had been turned upside down and, for the first time in history, the pagan religions were no longer in charge. "There is no greater drama in human record than the sight of a few Christians, scorned or oppressed by a succession of emperors, bearing all trials with a fierce tenacity, multiplying quietly, building order while their enemies generated chaos, fighting the sword with the word, brutality with hope, and at last defeating the strongest state that history has ever known. **Caesar and Christ had met in the arena, and Christ had won**" Christianity had been elevated to the **OFFICIAL RELIGION** of the Empire. [5]

The seeds to the rise of the Holy Roman Church started back in **378 A.D.** when the title of ***Pontifex Maximus – the official title for the***

---

[5] 1 Durant, Will, The Story Of Civilization, Caesar and Christ, Vol. 3, P. 652.

***high priest of the mysteries – was taken by the bishop of Rome.*** God immediately punished Rome because of this deceptive and insidious act. In **378 A.D.** the Roman army was soundly defeated for the first time, and their Emperor also perished in the battle. No one had defeated Rome in such a way for hundreds of years.

Augustine (354- 430 A.D.) is one of the church's great theologians. He may have unknowingly set the precedent on how the Holy Roman Catholic Church would deal with differences. In northern Africa a group of Christians known as the Donatists had challenged the church at Rome on one of their doctrines. The Donatists felt that, if a priest was secretly an unrepentant sinner, then those he had ministered to, be it marriage, communion, Baptism, etc., were invalid because of the priest's sin. Augustine's first response was to show them that their reasoning was faulty. When they would not recant, **Augustine's decision (414 A.D.) would haunt Christendom for the next thousand plus years.** His decision has been cited as the beginning of the Inquisition. He used the army of Rome to settle a theological decision. The Roman authorities confiscated Donatist property and assessed fines until the Donatists got back in line. **The Church at Rome had a new friend, Rome's power.**

The church had many bishops in various dioceses and they were all considered equal. This changed in **533 A.D.** In that year, *a decree was issued by the eastern Emperor, Justinian, elevating the bishop of Rome as "head of all the holy Churches, and of all the holy priests of God."* The first pope was to be Boniface III. Rome was a political empire that conquered people and land; whereas, the <u>**Holy Roman Church took possession of land, people, and souls.**</u>

Pope Innocent III in the 12th Century tried to exterminate every trace of resistance to Papal authority in Europe. Salvation was based on membership to the Holy Roman Catholic Church, tradition and works.

At the Third Lateran Council of **1179**, war was declared on all heretics (non-Catholics). Pope Alexander III decreed, at the Third Lateran Council, that Catholics were not to trade with heretics. Later, Pope Martin IV issued a decree preventing heretics from buying, selling, and owning property. If you did not bend your will to the popes you could not buy or sell.

The Inquisitions officially started in **1231**, even though it had been going on for hundreds of years.

*I Am, Therefore I Know*

A Catholic clergyman named John Wycliffe would begin to see that the Scriptures should be the property of all people. He decided to translate the whole Bible from **Latin into English**. He completed this around **1382**. This translation infected England with the Truth. The Catholic Church acted against this heretical movement and, in a few decades, stomped out most of the effects of Wycliffe's work and drove his followers underground.

**In 1425**, the Catholic Church, hoping to send a message to those who were thinking of committing treachery against the Holy Roman Church, ordered Wycliffe's bones exhumed and burned along with some two hundred books he had written.

**In 1478**, the Papacy began the **Spanish Inquisition**, wiping out virtually all Protestants (Protesters of the Holy Roman Catholic Church) in Spain by 1558.

A papal bull was issued in **1513** calling the remaining Bohemian brethren to present their cause before the Fifth Lateran Council. *No one appeared*. At the end of the council on May 5, 1514, Elliott writes, "The orator of the session ascended the pulpit; and, amidst the applause of the assembled council, uttered that memorable exclamation which… was never, I believe, pronounced before, and certainly never since – *'I am nemo reclamat, nullus obsistit'* – *'There is an end of resistance to the Papal rule and religion; opposers there exist no more'* and again *'The whole body of Christendom is now seen to be subjected to its Head [the Pope].'*" The Pope had a great festival to celebrate this supposed victory.

## THREE AND ONE HALF YEARS LATER ON OCTOBER 31st 1517, LUTHER NAILED THE 95 THESES TO THE DOOR OF THE WITTENBURG CHURCH!

Luther's 95 Theses were an indictment of the Holy Roman Catholic Church, declaring that its doctrines and traditions did not agree with the Bible.

Historians usually date the **start of the Protestant Reformation to the 1517** publication of Martin Luther's "95 Theses." The Reformation was a call to purify the church and a belief that the Bible, **not tradition nor the pope**, is be the sole source of spiritual authority. The Holy Roman Catholic Church did everything in **Latin**. This meant the uneducated masses were subject to the Church's understanding and interpretation of the Holy Scriptures. This obviously led to deception and abuse. Luther and the other reformers became the first to skillfully use the power of the printing press to get scripture in the hands of the masses in their languages.

The invention of the moveable type printing known as the Guttenberg Press around **1455**.

Printing of the Greek New Testament by Eramus in the year **1516**.

Printing of the first Swiss New Testament by Zwingli in the year **1518**.

Printing of the first German New Testament by Luther in **1522**.

Printing of the first English and Swedish Bibles by Tyndale in **1526**.

Printing in Italian in the year **1532**.

Printing of the Danish Bible in **1537**.

The Great Bible was commanded to be placed in every English church in **1539**.

The most well-known Bible started printing in **1611** - the King James Version.

The Bible would now be available to all in their language. Imagine if Luther had the next document. It is the Cardinals advising the Pope to make sure to never allow the people access to the Scriptures.

## Declaration of the Roman Catholic Cardinals To Pope Giulio III Carried in 1550.

"Of all the advice we can give to your holiness we have left the most necessary [most important] to the end. We must open our eyes well and use every effort available to us, and that is to allow the reading of the Gospel to be made as little as possible, [the Gospel, the truth is dangerous] especially in modern day language, [the common language other than Latin] in all those countries under our jurisdiction, to limit that part of the Gospel which is usually read during Mass, and to not allow any further reading of it. As long as the people are satisfied with such limitation [this is when someone else determines what you know] our interests will prosper, but as soon as the people want more, [the truth] our interests will fail. The Holy Bible is that book which more than anything has made [them] rise up against us those tumults and storms whose causes were lost. ***In fact, if anyone should accurately examine and compare the*** *teachings of the Bible with those made by our church [official Roman Catholic traditions and doctrines] he will soon find a difference, and comprehend that our teachings are often different from the Bible and even contrary to it.* [They are opposite of truth] If the people [Catholics] realize this they will make no objections to challenge us until everything comes to light and we will become the subject of mockery and universal hatred, *thus it is necessary to hide the Bible* [truth, the Gospel, will set you free] from the sight of the people but with extreme precautions so not to cause rebellions."

The Protestant Reformation met the full fury of the Holy Roman Catholic Church.

**The Church of England declared itself independent in 1529**, making England the first nation ever to break away from the Pope's strong grips. History shows that seven other entities (countries or provinces) broke from under the Pope's domination at this time. They were Holland, Zealand, Utrecht, Frieseland, Groningen, Overyssel, and Gutherland.

**In 1572**, on St. Bartholomew's Day, the Holy Roman Catholic Church *slaughtered up to 50,000 Protestants in one day*. In France, the French Protestants, known as the Huguenots, met severe opposition ending in a civil war that was halted only after the Pope issued the Edict of Toleration in 1598. This was just a part of the price that was paid by those who refused to accept what the official church had become – corrupt and unscriptural. The Holy Roman Church was drunk on the blood of the saints of God. H. Gratten Guinness states: **"It has been calculated that the Popes have, directly or indirectly, slain on account of their faith fifty-millions of martyrs."** The Church of Rome has shed more innocent Christian blood than any other institution in history. No historian would dispute this fact.

The major event in Europe directly impacting the Papacy in the year **1793** was the French Revolution. The King of France had been a solid source of support, even being referred to as "the eldest son of the church" by the Pope. France entered the Age of Reason. *Reason was the new god.* Law was passed on November 24, 1793, banning religious exercise. This included banning the Bible. It was the first time in the annals of history that a great nation had thrown off ALL religious principles and openly defied the power of heaven. Voltaire, the leader of the Enlightenment, declared the Bible was false. *What made the Bible appear false was the* *deception and misapplication by the Holy Roman Catholic Church.* As a result, France declared war on the ruling hierarchy. The power base of the Catholic Church would never recover. The revolution was aimed at the power of the Papacy. In five years, two million people were slain, including 24,000 priests. Forty thousand churches were made into stables. This was in France alone. Moral corruption, atheism, and dissolution of society spread throughout those countries where the Pope and his church were in power. This affected every Catholic nation in Europe.

**1793 A.D.** starts the deadliest contest for the mastery of the seas between Protestant England and Catholic Europe.

**1793**, Lord Hood crushes the French at Toulon.

**1794**, Lord Howe defeated the French at Ushant.

**1795**, Lord Bridgeport defeats the French and Dutch fleets at Cape Good Hope.

**1798**, the Spanish and Dutch are defeated off Cape St. Vincent and Campertown.

**1798**, Lord Nelson's victory over the French at the Nile.

**1801**, Lord Nelson's victory at Copenhagen.

**1805**, Lord's Nelson's annihilation of the French at Talfalgar are recorded.

**By 1805**, over 600 ships of the Line, Spain's largest war ships at that time, had been lost. This does not include the thousands of other vessels destroyed.

From 1796 to 1815, Napoleon was engaged in continuous war without a moment's cessation. Historian Dr. Keith writes on page 190 of <u>The Signs of the Times</u>, "Napoleon performed the miracles of genius. His achievements still dazzle, while they amaze the world. Within a space of eight years he scorched every kingdom in Europe, from Naples to Berlin, and from Lisbon to Moscow. Ancient kingdoms withered before the intense blaze of his power...Kingdoms were unsparingly rift like garments...like the sun, there was nothing hid from his great heat." *In 1815, the Congress at Vienna attempted to restore the old order, but the 380 principalities of pre-Napoleonic Europe would never reassemble again under the popes. All had been lost!*

**December 27, 1797**, Berthier, the commander of the French troops, received orders from the Directory to enter Italy and take Rome. The

French exceeded the Goths and Vandels in their pillaging of Rome's treasures. Rome's populace revolted as it, too, was swept up by the age of reason.

**In 1798**, Pope Pius VI was removed. ***The pope later died in exile at age 82.*** The historian Barnes writes, "In the year 1848, the pope was actually driven away to Gaeta, and... at this present time he is restored, though evidently with diminished power." Italian troops conquered Rome in 1870, and incorporated it back into the Kingdom of Italy.

Does the papacy change from using Latin and teaching that salvation is by the church, tradition and works? No, the papacy responds with ***non-scriptural*** declarations.

For example, in ***1854***, they issued the doctrine of the Immaculate Conception of Mary. They waited a long time to find this in Scripture. Oh, it is not there! Mary clearly acknowledged her need of a Savior for she proclaimed.

- <u>Luke 1:46-47</u>: "My soul doth magnify the Lord, and my spirit hath rejoiced in God my Savior."

***Mary knew that she was human and that she needed a Savior.*** Jesus was the Son of God and the Son of Man. He left heaven, took human form and felt temptation, pain, etc., just like we do. Mary needed to be human if Jesus was to be the Son of Man, as Scripture clearly says.

We currently know the Catholic Church as a post-Vatican II church. Today, the Vatican Church is a mere shadow of its former reach and control. The Catholic Church, the Papacy, the Vatican, and its hierarchy had absolute power over Europe for over 1,200 years.

**In 1964**, the Pope and the Vatican were forced under extreme pressure to put an end to many of the "mysteries." The "Declaration on Religious Freedom" of ***Vatican II*** was signed, sealed, and delivered by the Pope himself. The grand business in the papal communion was the performance of rites and ceremonies. Genuflections, crossings, burning of incense, processions, music, constitute the characteristic features of all papal churches. This is also when ***they stopped doing services in Latin and allowed the local language to be used.*** Today the Catholic Church really has two separate parts in struggle.

One is many local priests and members of the church, who continue to want more freedom and truth from the Scriptures taught. God sees only Christians, His children saved by faith in Christ, not saved by church membership and/or traditions. We are unified in Christ in spite of our theological differences.

The second part of the Catholic Church is the unrepentant hierarchy, whom God has asked to repent. *This terrible history is now our combined saga of the war for spiritual freedom, shared by both Protestants and Catholics. They survived only to bring the Good News to both Catholics and Protestants of our day.*

## THE RESPONSE TO THE HOLY ROMAN CATHOLIC CHURCH

*Calvin's doctrine of predestination of the elect, done completely by God, stood directly against the Holy Roman Catholic Church's error of salvation, which was "salvation by the Church" and doing works.* Once Calvin started the ball rolling, other Reformed theologians would be needed to find theological support from the Bible. Basically, Calvin's view of predestination said to the Holy Roman Catholic Church *that salvation is one hundred percent an act of God.* Humans have no role in the decision, including the Holy Roman Catholic Church. Before time, God chose what individuals would be saved and become part of the elect. At the same time, by default, those who are not saved are damned. When Calvin's starting point of the Reformed position is challenged, the typical response is that everyone deserves death followed by hell. If God, out of His mercy, has decided to give His grace, then who are we to question God for showing love to the chosen ones? *Once one takes the position that Salvation is by Election then you need to build the support system.*

By the Twentieth Century, to support this axiom, reformed theologians would create what became known as the "TULIP." T stood for Total Depravity, U stood for Unconditional election, L stood for Limited Atonement, I stood for Irresistible Grace, P stood for Perseverance of the Saints. The foundation of logical thinking is the **Law of Non-Contradiction**. This simply means something cannot be both true and not true at the same time and in the same respect. *You are either saved* *by faith or saved by election, but you cannot have them both.* Calvin's view of predestination eventually leads to what is known as **Double Predestination**, since the future of the elect and damned have been predetermined by God before time.

**Total Depravity** states man is unable, and would never, seek after God. Salvation is completely done by God alone, without man being involved.

**Unconditional election** is exactly as stated: one is chosen not based on anything but the choice of God.

**Limited atonement** teaches that God chose the elect only, and that salvation was not available for all.

**Irresistible Grace**, also known as effectual grace, supports double predestination because once God chooses, His grace is fully supported by the power of Almighty God. Who is more powerful than God?

**Perseverance of the Saints**: once God chooses, His will is unchangeable so those chosen will be part of the Bride of Christ. Some refer to this as "Once Saved, Always Saved."

## CHRISTIAN FIRST

God has a way of orchestrating our lives for His purposes. Being raised an atheist, and not having been exposed to the Bible, theology, doctrines, etc. meant that when I came to Christ at twenty-two years old I was, as they say, a "blank canvas." I had no preconceived ideas about the Bible and its doctrines. I only understood that it was the Word of God and all other information was subject to it, including science. When I read Genesis 1:1: "In the beginning God created the heavens and the earth," I realized evolution might not be true. I found out that only micro evolution within created families/species was allowed by God. (Chapter 3 of my first book Truth-Not Exactly). I received the Baptism of the Holy Spirit before I was told by theologians that it ended after the first century, along with the cessation of miracles. When you have no preconceived religious concepts, this allows one to read the Scriptures, and subsequently learn the doctrines, by reading all sides of each argument. All that matters is that the theology, doctrine, creed, etc., is compared *in context to the entire Scriptures.* I have not attended a formal Bible School. I have learned the Scriptures through depending on the Holy Spirit to teach me what the Scriptures have to say. Thankfully, God provided the right pastors, mentors and teachers throughout my life as a believer. My love of reading allowed me the pleasure of studying history along with the writings of great minds. I spent a year and a half in a non-denominational church. I spent thirty years in the Assembly of God denomination which is a non-reformed, evangelical, pentecostal church. When our youngest child went to medical school in Philadelphia, we attended a Presbyterian Church with her; a reformed church. When she moved to Detroit to continue her education, we started attending a reformed church near our home almost five years ago. We were invited by the pastor's wife, who grew up in the Assembly of God church we all attended together. Her father and I were Deacons together. My wife and I were at our present pastor's wedding years ago. That was the path that brought us to this reformed church.

After about two years, I was asked to be on the Session/Board. During the interview process it became apparent that I did not agree with all of the church's doctrine (non-essentials). This led me to ask for a hearing, which I was graciously granted. I would have twenty minutes to share. Leadership would then question me for twenty minutes, at which time I would leave and wait for their decision. During this hearing, I told them that I wanted be as transparent as I could about what I agreed with and/or disagreed with.

In summary, I told them I believed the Bible is the ultimate authority, I am a Creationist, I am not a Calvinist, I am not an Arminianist, I believe in God's Sovereignty – our will is subject to His will. I believe Jesus paid for **ALL** of our sins - not just the elect's. I believe in God's Predestination of events and control of all history. I believe in salvation by faith and I believe that God is a respecter of our free will when it comes to salvation. The questions that were asked revolved around one key issue: ***Salvation by Election versus Salvation by Faith*** - election of the individual before time, with everything else proceeding as a result of that. You can probably guess the resultant vote. It was unanimous! The following Sunday one of the individuals from the meeting came up to me and said that she got the point of what I shared at the hearing. I asked what she thought it was. Her response, ***"We are Christians before we are Presbyterians."*** She got it right! If I was successful in my communication, it meant all had to vote no - a yes vote would have, in essence, voted themselves off the session/board for agreeing with my exceptions. What surprised some of them who voted me off is that my relationship with each of them did not change. I still was their brother in Christ, still prayed with them, still loved them the same. *I gave them the right to be wrong; as long as it went both ways. We are not saved by correct doctrine. If that was true, then no one would ever be saved.* We are saved only by faith in Jesus Christ.

We joined this reformed church because it had three important attributes: first, excellent preaching and teaching of the Word; second, wonderful worship music and; finally, believers who were in love with Christ and loved one another.

- <u>Romans 14:1-5</u>: *"Accept the one whose faith [understanding added] is weak [different added], without quarreling over **disputable matters**.* One person's faith allows them to eat anything, but another, whose faith is weak, eats only vegetables. The one who eats everything must not treat with contempt the one who does not, and the one who does not eat everything must not judge the one who does, for God has accepted them. Who are you to judge someone else's servant? To their own master, servants stand or fall. And they will stand, for the Lord is able to make them stand. One person considers one day more sacred than another; another considers every day alike. ***Each of them should be fully convinced in their own mind.***"

It states not to quarrel **over disputable matters**. Our denomination has this as their motto: "In Essentials UNITY; In Non-Essentials LIBERTY; In all things LOVE." I continued serving and teaching in Sunday school classes and multiple small groups. When the disputable topics arise, I make sure that reformed, non-reformed and liberal positions are given equal explanation. Today, I am on the Deacon Board because I agree with the Essentials. The others know and accept my non-essential exceptions and they all agreed, in love, that I could serve and welcomed me accordingly.

## WHOSOEVER BY FAITH

***Redemption accomplished by Christ is unlimited***. Jesus' death on the cross is sufficient to cover everyone's sin. His sacrifice paid for all sin of all people and for all time. ***Redemption applied is limited***. Why? Because people with free will can choose not to believe and not to accept God's provision and Christ's payment for their sin!

- Romans 1:16: "For I am not ashamed of the gospel, because it is the ***power of God that brings salvation to everyone who believes***: first to the Jew, then to the Gentile."

Believe first then salvation comes.

- John 1:11-12: "He came to that which was his own, but his own did not receive him. Yet to all who did receive him, to those who ***believed in his name***, he ***gave the right*** to become children of God."

There are those who rejected and those who received. Those who believed in His Name, He gave them the gift of salvation. "Believed" is an action word; you must do something to become a child of God.

- John 3:18: "***Whoever believes*** in him is not condemned, but whoever does not believe stands ***condemned*** already because they have not ***believed in the name of God's one and only Son***."

This verse adds two additional truths: ***Whoever*** believes, which means anyone is able and is included; and the second, you must believe in God's one and only Son.

- John 3:16: "For God so loved ***the world*** that he gave his one and only Son, that ***whoever believes*** in him shall not perish but have eternal life."

Another "whoever believes" verse, but it has additional revelation: God so loved the world. ***The whole world means ALL of us.***

- 1 John 2:2: "He is the atoning sacrifice for our sins, and not only for ours but also for the sins of the ***whole world***."

This verse states the entire world.

- <u>2 Peter 3:9</u>: "The Lord is not slow in keeping his promise, as some understand slowness. Instead he is patient with you, ***not wanting anyone to perish, but everyone to come to repentance.***"

God does not want anyone to perish. In fact, it is His desire for *everyone* to come to repentance.

- <u>Romans 5:6-10</u>: "You see, at just the right time, when we were still powerless, ***Christ died for the ungodly.*** Very rarely will anyone die for a righteous person, though for a good person someone might possibly dare to die. ***But God demonstrates his own love for us in this: While we were still sinners, Christ died for us.*** Since we have now been justified by his blood, how much more shall we be saved from God's wrath through him! For if, ***while we were God's enemies***, we were reconciled to him through the death of his Son, how much more, having been reconciled, shall we be saved through his life!"

Christ died for the ungodly, sinners and God's enemies.

- <u>Job 36:5</u>: "God is mighty, ***but despises no one;*** he is mighty, and firm in his purpose."

Here is an interesting verse because damning people to hell, when they had no decision in it, would go counter to His own Word.

- <u>Acts 16:31</u>: "He then brought them out and asked, "Sirs, ***what must I do to be saved?*** They replied, ***"Believe in the Lord Jesus, and you will be saved...*"

Here we see again that salvation is about ***the choice and the action of believing*** in the Lord Jesus Christ.

- <u>Acts 17:30</u>: "In the past God overlooked such ignorance, but now He commands ***all people everywhere to repent.***"

He commands **all** people everywhere to repent. Again, another verse stating that all can come!

- Acts 20:21: "I have declared to both Jews and Greeks that they must turn to God in repentance and **have faith in our Lord Jesus.**"

Not only repent, but put faith in the correct place: the Lord Jesus.

- Hebrews 11:6: *"And without faith it is impossible to please God, because anyone who comes to him must believe that he exists and that he rewards those who earnestly seek him."*

We must have faith. Salvation depends on faith, our faith!

- Luke 7:50: "Jesus said to the woman, '***Your faith has saved you***; go in peace.'"

Whose faith? A person's faith.

- Romans 4:5: "However, to the one who does not work but trusts God who justifies the ungodly, ***their faith*** is credited as righteousness."

Whose faith? Their faith.

- Matthew 9:2: "Some men brought to him a paralyzed man, lying on a mat. When Jesus saw ***their faith***, he said to the man, 'Take heart, son; your sins are forgiven.'"

Whose faith? Their faith. We were created by God with the ability to make decisions. Many daily decisions require a step of faith. Based on what we believe, we then act. It is how human's process input and choose, using our God-given free will.

- Ephesians 2:8-9: "*For it is by* grace you have been saved, through faith - and this is not from yourselves, *it is the gift of God - not by works,* so that no one can boast."

We have been saved by grace. This means that salvation is a gift of God. It was His idea before time and creation, that God would do all the work. His Son would pay the price so that this gift of God could be available for those who, *by faith,* receive the gift of salvation freely from an all-loving God. The question: Is faith a work? Not according to the verse just read. *Your faith does not change it from being a gift of God.*

- Romans 3:26-27: "He [Jesus added] did it to demonstrate his righteousness at the present time, so as to be just and *the one who justifies those who have faith in Jesus. Where, then, is boasting? It is excluded…*"

Who justified us? Only Christ can do that work.

- Galatians 3:11: "Clearly no one who *relies on the law [works added]* is justified before God, because **the righteous will live by faith.**"

Works cannot save us. This verse states we are saved by faith. According to this verse, that is clearly not a "WORK." So, "by faith" is just the act of receiving a gift, which is no more meritorious than a beggar receiving a handout.

- James 1:17: "Every good and *perfect gift is from above*, coming down from the Father of the heavenly lights, who does not change like shifting shadows."

Who deserves the credit for the Gift; the giver or the receiver? The one who gives it! In summary, from the above verses we see the following truths:

1) God brings salvation to everyone. Some reject the offer and some accept the offer.

2) It is their God given choice of being granted free will in the decision of repentance and acceptance of Jesus.
3) Those who believe on the name of Jesus Christ receive the gift of salvation.
4) This gift is for the whole world and all are given a choice to make.
5) Their faith is what brings salvation.
6) Salvation is by grace and is a gift of God and not of any man's works.
7) Salvation is offered to all sinners and to His enemies freely.
8) Faith is not a work.
9) We must exercise our faith and choose to believe in the one Name that can save, the Lord Jesus Christ.

## TOTAL DEPRAVITY

Total Depravity means man is so depraved that he will not seek God, nor is he capable of responding to God in faith. Basically, he can do nothing about his future, thus he has no hope.

- Ephesians 2:1-2: "As for you, **you were dead in your transgressions and sins**, in which you used to live when you followed the ways of this world and of **the ruler** [Satan added] **of the kingdom of the air**, the spirit who is now at work in those who are disobedient."

We are dead spiritually because of sin and our father is Satan. These first two verses sound very supporting of total depravity, which is why they are pointed to by those who say man is unable to help himself, or choose Christ. Total depravity require election first, followed by regeneration and then faith, even though-as you have read above-the order is always faith followed by regeneration.

- Ephesians 2:3-5: "**All of us** also lived among them at one time, gratifying the cravings of our flesh and following its desires and thoughts. **Like the rest**, we were by nature deserving of wrath. But because of His great love for us, God, who is rich in mercy, **made us alive, with Christ even when we were dead in transgressions** it is by grace you have been saved."

This is written to the believer. The two verses can be understood in context of the entire section. Note that God makes us alive even though we were dead. How?

- <u>Ephesians 2:6-10</u>: "And God raised us up with Christ and seated us with him in the heavenly realms in Christ Jesus, in order that in the coming ages he might show the incomparable riches of his grace, expressed in his kindness to us in Christ Jesus. ***For it is by grace you have been saved, through faith*** - and this is not from yourselves, ***it is the gift of God*** not by works, so that no one can boast. For we are ***God's handiwork***, created in Christ Jesus to do good works, which God prepared in advance for us to do."

Once we read all eight verses; we see the answer. Those who are dead are brought back to life because of Christ being raised. God is able to raise us due to His Grace by faith. Whose faith? ***Those who are dead in sin.***

Why are we sinners? The first reason is that God condemned all mankind because of Adam and Eve. How do we know that the sin of Adam has made us all sinners? The Bible clearly states that death is a result of disobedience (sin) to God. Adam and Eve ate from the tree of Good and Evil knowing the penalty was death. The Bible states surely they would die. Adam and Eve did – not immediately, but eventually. Everyone has died since them, other than a few select exceptions (Jesus ascended after His resurrection, Enoch and Elisha were both taken up to heaven). Death is upon each human ever born and this fact ties us to Adam and his curse of death. Why should my fate be determined by Adam's sin and God's decision about it? Why shouldn't I, each of us, start off perfect and see what happens? Two reasons revealed themselves: First, every human would eventually fail. Why? There is precedent. Adam and Eve, who were perfect, failed. God knew the result would be our failure. He is all-knowing and, therefore, prepared a better plan. ***By condemning all with Adam, God's genius is revealed.*** God could redeem all of us by the last Adam - Jesus Christ! The second reason is that we each have a propensity to sin - we run to it. I know this goes against what many want to believe, which is that man is basically good. Let's see what the Word of God states:

- Genesis 6:5: "The LORD saw how great the wickedness of the **human race** had become on the earth, and that every inclination of the thoughts of the human heart was **only evil all the time**."

- Job 15:11-16: "Are God's consolations not enough for you, words spoken gently to you? Why has your heart carried you away, and why do your eyes flash, so that you vent your rage against God and **pour out such words** from your mouth?"

What are mortals, that they could be pure, or those born of woman, that they could be righteous? If God places no trust in his holy ones, if even the heavens are not pure in his eyes, how much less **mortals, who are vile and corrupt, who drink up evil like water!**'"

- Romans 3:12: "**All** have turned away, they have together become worthless; there is **no one who does good**, not even one."

- Romans 3:23: "…for **all have sinned** and fall short of the glory of God."

- 1 John 1:8: "If we claim **to be without sin, we deceive ourselves** and the truth is not in us."

We could go on and on. This brings us to a discussion of the **propensity (tendency) to sin** versus **the necessity (no choice) to sin.** The Bible teaches us that we have a propensity to sin. However, it is **our choice** to sin which is why God can **hold us accountable**. If sinning was by necessity and we have no choice, then God would be unjust to condemn humans. Total Depravity, where man is helpless without His God-given right to choose (free will), goes against the God of the Bible's revelation of Himself to us. **Can a good God create creatures who are without hope because they truly have no choice in the fact they will sin?** Or, will they then be condemned to hell for eternity because it was a necessity beyond their control or choice? There is no argument that we humans can become depraved. The Scriptures clearly say we can.

*I Am, Therefore I Know*

- Romans 1:25-32: "They ***exchanged*** [a choice added] the truth about God for a lie, and worshiped and served created things rather than the Creator—who is forever praised. Amen. Because of this, God gave them over to shameful lusts. Even their women ***exchanged*** natural sexual relations for unnatural ones. In the same way the men also ***abandoned*** natural relations with women and were inflamed with lust for one another. Men committed shameful acts with other men, and received in themselves the due penalty for their error. Furthermore, just as they did not think it worthwhile to retain the knowledge of God, so **God gave them over to a depraved mind**, so that they do what ought not to be done. They have become filled with every kind of wickedness, evil, greed and depravity. They are full of envy, murder, strife, deceit and malice. They are gossips, slanderers, God-haters, insolent, arrogant and boastful; they invent ways of doing evil; they disobey their parents; they have no understanding, no fidelity, no love, no mercy. **Although they know God's righteous decree that those who do such things deserve death**, they not only ***continue*** [a choice added] to do these very things but also ***approve*** of those who practice them."

They exchanged and abandoned - **<u>both are by choice</u>**. Then, God gave them over to a depraved mind. However, even with a depraved mind Scripture clearly states that **they still know God's righteous decrees and that they chose not to continue in them and approved of others doing the same.** No matter how depraved one is, God placed knowledge of Him (Rom 1:20), and wrote His laws on our hearts (Rom 2:14), No one is **<u>not able</u>** to respond to God's offer. God's Holy Spirit will need to draw them (woo). They will need to hear the Word of God, they will need the Holy Spirit to awaken them. He can open eyes, ears and even illuminate the mind, while tugging on their hears, so that no matter where they are they may **"PERHAPS"** *choose* of their own free will by faith to believe on the only name that can save: JESUS CHRIST! The question is, and remains, can anyone's sins - no matter how many and how evil - make them not qualified to be saved? ***The worst of us can, and have been, saved by the***

*Blood of Jesus Christ. This I know. What are the limits of God's grace? Does any human know?*

## <u>UNCONDITIONAL ELECTION</u>

Unconditional election of individuals by God before time began fails for multiple reasons. *First, it goes against who God has revealed Himself to be in the Bible.* God being Good, Loving and Just is unable to create humans for the sole purpose of sending them to hell for eternity. You could ask any twelve year old with a sibling: Would it be fair if God decided before you were born that one of you goes to heaven and the other goes to hell? This is the position of individual unconditional election before time. If salvation by unconditional election is true, then why preach salvation by faith since it does not change who was selected by God before time? *Second, there are no verses regarding salvation by election stating that personal salvation is directed at the individual level. It must be created by inference, interpretation and assumption using complex rationales.* God predestined at the corporate level. He predestined the Bride of Christ, made up of the elect (individuals). He chose <u>*us*</u> - plural.

- <u>Ephesians 1:4-5</u>: "For *he chose us* [note: us - plural, not I] *in him before the creation* of the world to be holy and blameless in his sight. In love *He predestined <u>us</u> for adoption to sonship through Jesus Christ*, in accordance with his pleasure and will."

He chose <u>*us*</u> and predestined us for adoption. How are <u>*we*</u> adopted? Through faith in Jesus Christ. How do we acquire Christ by faith using our free will?

- <u>Ephesians 1:11-12</u>: "In him <u>*we*</u> [note: we – plural, not I] were also *chosen*, having *been predestined according to the plan* of him who works out everything in conformity with the purpose of his will, in order that <u>*we*</u>, who were the first to *put our hope in Christ*, might be for the praise of his glory."

*Again using our free will; we choose to put our hope by faith in Christ.* What really is predestined, according to God's plan, is that there would be a Bride of Christ made up of the elect who by faith chose Christ. Election is **<u>UNCONDITIONAL from God's viewpoin</u>**t; but it is **<u>CONDITIONAL to me and you</u>!** God is the "I AM." He knows who are the elect. That is why He can make statements like "I will not lose any!" *All verses that contain words such as predestined, called, etc. need to be understood in context of the "I AM" and the whole of Scripture.* There is no doctrine clearer in the Bible than salvation by faith.

## <u>LIMITED ATONEMENT</u>

Limited atonement teaches that God chose the elect only, and that salvation was not available for all. Theologians needed to create this to support the Salvation by election. This falls apart quickly because the Scriptures are loaded with verses that say Jesus died for all sin. Jesus came to save the world, to give His life for many, and **Whosoever** may come.

- <u>John 3:16-17</u>: "For God so loved the world that he gave his one and only Son, that **whoever** believes in him shall not perish but have eternal life. For God did not send his Son into the world to condemn the world, but **to save the world** through him."

One of the most well-known verses in the Bible says it quite clearly.

- <u>1 Timothy 2:1-6</u>: "I urge, then, first of all, that petitions, prayers, intercession and **thanksgiving be made for all people**— for kings and all those in authority, that we may live peaceful and quiet lives in all godliness and holiness. This is good, and pleases God our Savior, **who wants all people to be saved** and to come to a knowledge of the truth. For there is one God and one mediator between God and mankind, the man Christ Jesus, **who gave himself as a ransom for all people**. This has now been witnessed to at the proper time."

Again, prayers for all - not just the elect. **God our Savior wants all people saved.** Why would this need to be stated if it is conditional? This Scripture tells us that it is not settled who is going to be the elect. God is in the process of doing everything in His power to redeem all. Act 17:26-27 states God chose where and when we should live so He could orchestrate our lives for one thing: that **"PERHAPS"** we would chose Christ.

## IRRESISTIBLE GRACE

Irresistible grace means that, if God decided you were part of the elect, He then used irresistible grace to regenerate you so that you would be saved. Many prefer irresistible grace to be referred to as effectual grace, since it sounds nicer, although the outcome is the same. At the end of the day, ***irresistible grace is a form of fatalism and removes man from the equation, making history nothing more than a meaningless script.*** Yet, the prophets of God brought warnings. Depending on the people's responses, they received punishment and destruction or, if they repented, received His blessings. Decisions people make are in their control. How can God hold anyone accountable for actions if they are not free? As people exercised their God-given free will, it somehow fit into the general and grand scheme of God's unfolding master plan for history. The how and why each person's individual decisions can work into God's overall plan is known exclusively by the Divine. **God is never EXCLUSIVE.** Religion can be exclusive, man-made traditions can be exclusive; and man-made doctrines can be exclusive. **The God of the Bible is an INCLUSIVE GOD = *"whosoever will."***

## PERSEVERANCE OF THE SAINTS

Perseverance of the Saints, understood as part of the TULIP, believes that those who are elected before time are guaranteed from falling away; thus, salvation is eternal and absolutely secure. This is where we get the saying "Once saved always saved" comes from.

Our discussion will include perseverance of the saints, backsliding and apostasy. We will start with passages on assurance.

- John 5:24: "Very truly I tell you, whoever ***hears my word and believes*** Him who sent me [Jesus] ***has eternal life*** and will not be judged but has ***crossed over from death to life.***"

Whoever hears and believes has now crossed over from death to life.

- 1 John 5:13: "I write these things to you **who believe** in the name of the Son of God so that you **may know** that you have eternal life."

You need to know that you already have eternal life.

- Ephesians 1:13-14: "And you also were included in Christ when you heard the message of truth, the gospel of your salvation. When you **believed,** you were **marked in him with a seal, the promised Holy Spirit**, who is a deposit guaranteeing our inheritance until the redemption of those who are God's possession—to the praise of his glory."

When we receive Christ, the **Holy Spirit seals us**, sets us apart.

- Romans 8:16: "***The Spirit himself testifies with our spirit that we are God's children.***"

At the same time His Spirit witnesses to our spirit that we are God's children by adoption.

- Philippians 1:4-6: "In all my prayers for all of you, I always pray with joy because of your partnership in the gospel from the first day until now, **being confident** of this, that **He who began a good work in you will carry it on to completion** until the day of Christ Jesus."

God is our source of confidence. He has promised to do all that He can to insure that we finish.

- 2 Timothy 1:12: "That is why I am suffering as I am. Yet this is no cause for shame, because I know whom I have believed, and am convinced that ***He is able to guard what I have entrusted to him until that day.***"

Jesus is able to guard what we entrusted (our salvation, our future) to Him.

- John 10:27-29: "My sheep listen to my voice; I know them, and they follow me. I give them eternal life, and they shall never perish; **no one will snatch them out of my hand**. My Father, who has given them to me, is greater than all; **no one can snatch them out of my Father's hand.**"

No one means No One!

- John 6:39: "And this is the will of him who sent me, that ***I shall lose none of all those he has given me,*** but raise them up at the last day."

None will be lost, He is the "I AM" and he knows. Romans 8:35-39, as discussed earlier, states that no power in the universe can separate us from the love of God.

- 2 Timothy 2:13: "...*if we are faithless*, He remains faithful, for He cannot disown himself."

- Jude 24-25: "To Him who is able to ***keep you from stumbling*** and to present you before His glorious presence without fault and with great joy - to the only God our Savior be glory, majesty, power and authority, through Jesus Christ our Lord, before all ages, now and forevermore! Amen."

These are promises provided to the believers to remind them that their salvation cannot be taken away by someone else or some other power. God is faithful to us even when we are not faithful to Him. He is the God of love as revealed to us in Scripture. Since God is the "I AM," then He knows all. That is why He can make statements like ***"I shall lose none."*** Remember, for God, the elect are known from before time.

Scripture reveals, for a believer, evidences that we are truly His!

- 1 John 2:3: "We know that we have come to know him if we ***keep His commands***."

- <u>1 John 2:5-6</u>: "But if anyone **obeys His word, love for God is truly made complete** in them. This is how we know we are in Him: Whoever claims to live in Him must live as Jesus did."

- <u>1 John 3:14</u>: "We know that we have passed from death to life, **because we love each other.** Anyone who does not love remains in death."

- <u>1 John 5:18</u>: "Dear children, let us not love with words or speech but **with actions** and in truth."

- <u>1 John 5:24</u>: "The one who **keeps God's commands** lives in Him, and he in them. And this is how we know that He lives in us: **We know it by the Spirit he gave us.**"

- <u>1 John 4:11-13</u>: "Dear friends, since God so loved us, we also ought **to love one another.** No one has ever seen God; but if we love one another, God lives in us and His love is made complete in us. **This is how we know that we live in Him and He in us**: He has given us of his Spirit."

Notice that the evidences of true spiritual living show up as **obedience to the Word of God and to Jesus**, along with a love that goes beyond words and then turns into action, which is undergirded by truth. When we look at verses on assurance, we can know today that we are saved and that we have been **sealed by receiving the Holy Spirit** and are assured that God will do His part in helping us to retain eternal salvation. The Scriptures provide ample verses for self-evaluation. The three stages of growth are Infancy (babes), Adolescence (young) and adulthood (mature).

- <u>1 Peter 2:2</u>: "Like newborn babies, **crave pure spiritual milk**, so that by it you may grow up in your salvation."

Infancy requires nourishment from God's Word, Encouragement, Support, Instruction and - most of all - Love from God's people.

- <u>1 John 2:14</u>: "I write to you, dear children, because you know the Father. I write to you, fathers, because you know him who is from the beginning. I write to you, **young men [Adolescence added], because you are strong, and the word of God lives in you**, and you have overcome the evil one."

Adolescents accept God's Word as truth. They are learning to be obedient to it. They lean more and more on God and rely on His promises.

- <u>Ephesians 3:16-19</u>: "I pray that out of his glorious riches He may strengthen you with power through His Spirit in your inner being, so that Christ may dwell in your hearts through faith. And I pray that you, **being rooted and established in love**, may have power, together with all the Lord's holy people, to grasp how wide and long and high and deep is the love of Christ, and **to know this love that surpasses knowledge** - that you may be filled to the measure of all the fullness of God."

The mature believer (adulthood) is one who personally experiences the love of Christ in his/her life, which surpasses knowledge of God and Jesus. Mature believers commune with their Lord.

- <u>1 Peter 1:22</u>: "Now that you have **purified yourselves by obeying the truth** so that you have **sincere love for each other, love one another deeply, from the heart**."

Communion with Christ is seen in believers' lives by their heartfelt love for each other. God has promised us a new heart, one full of love.

- <u>Ephesians 4:14:</u> "Then we will no longer be infants, **tossed back and forth by the waves**, and **blown here and there by every wind of teaching** and by the **cunning and craftiness of people** in their deceitful scheming."

Mature believers should not be emotionally impacted by the events of the world. They should know that the daily news events are just blips and, at the end of the day, God is still sovereign. They are under the protection of the God of this universe. The final evidence that one is truly a believer is the slow and steady acquisition of the fruit of the Spirit as described in

- Galatians 5:22-23: "But the fruit of the Spirit is love, joy, peace, forbearance, kindness, goodness, faithfulness, gentleness and self-control. Against such things there is no law."

Is present assurance in itself a guarantee of ultimate eternal salvation? Looking at Scripture we find that there are warnings. This important and often overlooked verse is written to believers:

- 1 John 5:13-16: "I write these things to you **who believe in the name of the Son of God** [believers added] so that you may know that **you have eternal life**. This is the confidence we have in approaching God: that if we ask anything according to His will, he hears us. And if we know that He hears us - whatever we ask - we know that we have what we asked of Him. *If you see any brother or sister commit a sin that does not lead to death*, you should pray and God will give them life. I refer to those whose sin does not lead to death. *There is a sin that leads to death...*"

There is a warning here about sin in a believer's life. Certain sins do not lead to death; they lead to backsliding. However, Scripture warns the believer the there is a sin that leads to death, or apostasy.

The Old Testament uses the term "backsliding" to speak of those who have been near to God but have allowed sin to take them away from Him.

- Jeremiah 14:7: "Our **backsliding** is great; we have sinned against you."

- Jeremiah 2:19: "'Your wickedness will punish you; your **backsliding** will rebuke you. Consider then and realize how evil and bitter it is for you when *you forsake the Lord your God and have no awe of me*,' declares the Lord, the Lord Almighty."

Backsliding can be caused by many things. Whatever the sin might be that leads us away from God, it must be dealt with honestly and brought before Him in repentance. God loves us and wants us to be close to Him. Even when we sin against Him, He promises to forgive.

- <u>Hosea 14:4</u>: "I will heal their waywardness and love them freely, for my anger has turned away from them."

When we backslide, not if we backslide, the Holy Spirit warns us. God will send help through people in our lives. It is an important truth to know all can backslide. What is more important is what to do when it we backslide. Earlier, I shared about David and His sin. What did He do? Repent and confess.

- <u>1 John 1:9</u>: *"If we confess our sins, He is faithful and just and will forgive us our sins and purify us from all unrighteousness."*

I remember telling our Sunday school students after they had become believers that they **could no longer be successful sinners.** They now had the Holy Spirit who would not let them enjoy sin like before they accepted Christ.

I have been sent to different brothers in Christ for the purpose of restoration. This is a very hard thing to do, and must be done in love with the help of the Holy Spirit. I remember having a talk with a new believer who was unfaithful to his wife. This man could have been a male model. With regularity, his job put him contact with new women who, according to him, would throw themselves at him. I asked him a very simple question: "How many times would you have to cheat to be an adulterer?" He knew the answer. His choice was simple. Who was going to be his master? He chose correctly and today he and his wife have been happily married more than twenty-five years. Backsliding is about us separating ourselves from God because some idol/sin has captured our attention. It always starts small and unsuspecting. I have had periods in my life where I have cooled off in my walk and love of Christ. I thank God for His faithfulness, His Holy Spirit's constant tugging, and the people God has placed in my life. Each has been for my benefit. ***I need all the help that He promised!***

What happens to backsliders who will not repent? They continue in sin. If you put a frog in a pan of cool water, he will just sit there. If you slowly heat it up, the frog does not know his death is coming. It is the same in the spiritual life of a person. Sin separates us from God. At some point, we can become an apostate. An apostate is someone who renounces their former belief in Christ.

- Hebrews 10:26-29: "***If we deliberately keep on sinning*** after we have received the knowledge of the truth, no sacrifice for sins is left, but only a fearful expectation of judgment and of raging fire that will consume the enemies of God. Anyone who rejected the law of Moses died without mercy on the testimony of two or three witnesses. How much more severely do you think someone deserves to be punished ***who has trampled the Son of God underfoot, who has treated as an unholy thing the blood of the covenant that sanctified them, and who has insulted the Spirit of grace?***"

The Scriptures clearly teach that an apostate is someone ***who counts the blood of Christ as common, not divine, or unholy.*** He or she no longer sees Christ as the Son of God, and His sacrifice on the cross the only and necessary payment for their sin.

- Hebrews 6:4-6: "It is impossible for those who have once ***been enlightened***, who have ***tasted the heavenly gift***, who have ***shared in the Holy Spirit***, who have ***tasted the goodness*** of the word of God and the powers of the coming age ***and who have fallen away***, to be brought back to repentance. To their loss they are crucifying the Son of God all over again and subjecting him to public disgrace."

- Hebrews 2:1-4: "We must pay the most careful attention, therefore, to what we have heard, ***so that we do not drift away.*** For since the message spoken through angels was binding, and every violation and disobedience received its just punishment, how shall we escape if we ignore so great a salvation? This salvation, which was first announced by the Lord, was confirmed to us by those who heard him. God also testified to it by signs, wonders and various miracles, and by gifts of the Holy Spirit distributed according to his will."

**Why tell me to pay attention? Because I can drift away.**

- II Peter 2:18-22: "'For they mouth empty, boastful words and, by appealing to the lustful desires of the flesh, they entice people who are just escaping from those who live in error. They promise them freedom, while they themselves are slaves of depravity—for people are slaves to whatever has mastered them. *If they have escaped the corruption of the world by knowing our Lord and Savior Jesus Christ and are again entangled in it and overcome, <u>they are worse off at the end</u> than they were at the beginning. It would have been better for them not to have known the way of righteousness, than to have known it and then to turn their backs on the sacred command that was passed on to them.* Of them the proverbs are true: 'A dog returns to its vomit,' and, 'A sow that is washed returns to her wallowing in the mud.'"

They knew the right way and then chose to return back to their old master.

- Luke 8:13: "Those on the rocky ground are the ones **who receive the word** with joy when they hear it, but they have no root. **They believe for a while**, but in the time of testing **they fall away**.

***In one verse, <u>Luke 8:13</u>, Jesus states "they believe" and "they fall away."*** These Scriptures provide the whole picture concerning preservation of the saints. God will uphold His promise while, at the same time, respecting our free will. **Sometimes I wish I could be <u>an editor</u> of the Bible.** This way I could ignore many of the hard truths found in Scripture. However, it is always better to know all when it is my/our soul that is on the line.

I have personally been impacted by apostasy. My best man, whom I shared about earlier, was a Christian when I knew him forty plus years ago. Some time ago, he had stopped by on one of his business trips. As we talked, he shared with me that he was no longer a Christian. He said: "I no longer need the crutch of Christianity." As we continued talking, it became quite clear what happened. After he left the USAF, he joined the Navy and became an F-14 Navigator. Everyone on an aircraft carrier knows that the thousands of support personnel are there for one reason: so the pilots with their navigators can fulfill their mission. They are treated like gods. When he left the Navy, he became very successful and saw himself as a self-made success story. Was my best man's success bad in and of itself? No. I gave him a copy of my first book <u>Truth-Not Exactly</u> and told him that I would be praying for him, my good friend. Right now, I wait upon the Lord for his phone call one day!

- <u>2 Peter 3:17</u>: "Therefore, dear friends, since you have **been forewarned**, be on your guard so that you may not be carried away by the error of the lawless and ***fall from your secure position***."

God, in love, has told us in His Holy Scriptures to be on guard, because our Great Salvation is secure from every power in the universe except one. My God-given, God-respected, God-protected FREE WILL!

## Chapter 9

# MORE THAN A FAN

The dictionary says a Fan is "an enthusiastic admirer." Fans cheer loudest when things are going great, but most walk away when things go south. Fans sit safely in the stands, or at home in front of the TV, but they know nothing of the sacrifice and pain of the field. The question is: am I willing to get in the game, or do I prefer sitting on the bench? I love the commercial on TV where the football player/champion has his team uniform on and is sitting next to a fan dressed identically. The punch line is to call the number shown and you, too, can have any uniform from any team without any of the sacrifice or pain, like the football player/champion. I, like most others, want the benefits that come with God without any real commitment/sacrifice to God. As they say, I prefer to have my cake and eat it, too. As I read the Scriptures, God states His first and greatest commandment in:

- Matthew 22:36-37: "Teacher, which is the greatest commandment in the Law? Jesus replied: *'Love the Lord your God with all your heart and with all your soul and with all your mind.'*

This is to love God to the exclusion of all other gods.

- Exodus 20:3: "*You shall have no other gods before me.*"

God must be first, which means Jesus must be first, and the Holy Spirit must be allowed to transform me.

- <u>1 Peter 1:3-11</u>: "His divine power has **given us everything we need for a godly life** through our knowledge of him who called us by his own glory and goodness. Through these he has **given us His very great and precious promises**, so that through them you **may participate in the divine nature**, having escaped the corruption in the world caused by evil desires. For this very reason, make every effort to ***add to your faith*** goodness; and to goodness, knowledge; and to knowledge, self-control; and to self-control, perseverance; and to perseverance, godliness; and to godliness, mutual affection; and to mutual affection, love. **For if you possess these qualities in increasing measure, they will keep you from being ineffective and unproductive** in your knowledge of our Lord Jesus Christ. But whoever does not have them is nearsighted and blind, forgetting that they have been cleansed from their past sins. Therefore, my brothers and sisters, make every effort to confirm your calling and election. For if you do these things, **you will never stumble, and you will receive a rich welcome into the eternal kingdom of our Lord and Savior Jesus Christ.**"

Scripture tells us that He has given me everything I need. I am to start in ***Faith***, then add goodness, knowledge, self-control, perseverance, godliness, mutual affection, and love in increasing amounts over my lifetime. If I choose to obey the Scriptures, I will receive a rich welcome into the eternal kingdom of our Lord. **If** is the biggest word in the dictionary. When I chose Christ by faith that was just the starting point. If I had died five minutes later I would be like the thief on the cross - good to go. However, I - like most - now have to live out my faith in Christ.

- <u>James 2:20-22</u>: "You foolish person, do you want evidence that faith without deeds is useless? Was not our father Abraham considered righteous for what he did when he offered his son Isaac on the altar? ***You see that his faith and his actions were working together, and his faith was made complete by what he did.***"

I had to make a decision to be more than a Fan. ***Was I going to be a disciple?*** Was I going to get in the game? There is a price for either decision. A non-decision is still a decision. I understood the price when I read:

- Matthew 24:13: "but the **one who stands firm to the end will be saved**."

Scripture paints it as a road few choose.

- Matthew 7:14: "But small is the gate and narrow the road that leads to life, and only a few find it."

I have to choose where my treasure will be.

- Matthew 6:19-20: "Do not store up for yourselves treasures on earth, where moths and vermin destroy, and where thieves break in and steal. But store up for yourselves treasures in heaven, where moths and vermin do not destroy, and where thieves do not break in and steal. Do not let the world mold you."

The Bible is clear when it warns us where your treasure is, so is our heart.

- Matthew 6:21: "*For where your treasure is, there your heart will be also.*"

- Jeremiah 17:10: "*I the LORD search the heart and examine the mind, to reward each person according to their conduct, according to what their deeds deserve.*"

This is one of the most important verses on how God will judge what we have done. We have to be concerned not only with doing the correct action, but why we do it is even more important!

So far, I understood God wanted me to put Him first. He has provided all I need. I am to add to my faith and grow constantly. I should show my faith by doing the works God wants me to do with the correct motives.

The location of my treasure reveals where my heart really is. But there is another important requirement.

- Matthew 7:21-23: "Not everyone who says to me, 'Lord, Lord,' will enter the kingdom of heaven, but only the one who does the will of my Father who is in heaven. Many will say to me on that day, 'Lord, Lord, did we not prophesy in your name and in your name drive out demons and in your name perform many miracles?' Then I [Jesus] will tell them plainly, *'I never knew you. Away from me, you evildoers!'*"

Jesus wants us to know Him. When we look at the Hebrew word "yada," we get more of a feel of what is desired by Christ. Yada means "***To know completely and to be known completely.***" It goes even further. One Hebrew scholar says it is like "***a mingling of the souls.***" The closest relationship I have here on earth is my marriage. My wife knows me only second to God. Yet, with all my shortcomings and failures, she chooses to still love me. God wants more than that from me. My wife can't read my mind or see my motives like Jesus can. It is my choice to engage in this intimate relationship as His Bride. God's offer of relationship is available to all, and is necessary, according to Scripture. ***These words of Jesus have caused me more self-examination than any other verse in the Bible.***

I want what Paul tells Timothy that he is longing as in:

- 2 Timothy 4:7-8: "I have fought the good fight, I have finished the race, I have kept the faith. Now there is in store for me the crown of righteousness, which the Lord, the righteous Judge, will award to me on that day - and not only to me, but also to all who have longed for his appearing."

Will it be worth it? Listen, and you tell me.

- Revelation 3:21: "To the one who is victorious, ***I will give the right to sit with me on my throne***, just as I was victorious and sat down with my Father on his throne."

I do not understand how it will work, but I like the sound of it!

- <u>1 Corinthians 3:11-15</u>: "***For no one can lay any foundation other than the one already laid, which is Jesus Christ.*** If anyone builds on this foundation using gold, silver, costly stones, wood, hay or straw, ***their work will be shown for what it is***, because the day will bring it to light. It will be revealed with fire, and the fire will ***test the quality of each person's work***. If what has been built ***survives, the builder will receive a reward***. If it is burned up, the builder will suffer loss but yet will be saved—even though only as one escaping through the flames."

Only what is done out of love and in the power of the Holy Spirit for the building of the Kingdom of God will survive. On that day if I receive anything, I know, like my salvation, it was by grace. The same for any crowns. They too are by grace, which is why I, and all who receive them, will lay them at the feet of Christ, Lord of All!

***If you could be king for a day*** what would you want, do and/or change. Many of us have thought about it, less have said it out loud. Our answer would reveal much. Take a moment and think: what if?

**To those who do not know Christ and consider themselves enlightened/intellectuals:**

We live in a time when individuals can have it their way. All is available and all is acceptable. There is no longer anything wrong. What was wrong only a decade or two ago, is now being championed as good. Is God surprised by this? No, listen to Scripture and hear about our time.

- <u>2 Timothy 4:3-4</u>: "***For the time will come when people will not put up with sound doctrine. Instead, to suit their own desires, they will gather around them a great number of teachers to say what their itching ears want to hear. They will turn their ears away from the truth and turn aside to myths.***"

Television today has a channel for whatever one wants to see or hear. This is a reflection of the times in which we live.

**To those who were once part of the Jesus Christ, our Savior's Church, come home!**

- Galatians 1:6-8: "I am astonished that you are so quickly deserting the one who called you to live in the grace of Christ and *are turning to a different gospel - which is really no gospel at all.* Evidently some people are throwing you into confusion and are trying to pervert the gospel of Christ. But even if we or an angel from heaven should preach a gospel other than the one we preached to you, let them be under God's curse!"

Don't let anyone keep you from reading and hearing the Word of God. It is good for what ails us. There are no "Lone Rangers" in heaven. We all need the body of Christ in our lives more than we even know. God loves you and wants you back.

**To the Liberal Theologians and Revisionist Historians, stop teaching what you truly do not understand!**

Liberal Theologians have used Higher Criticism to review the Bible as if it is like any common book. Higher Criticism means nothing more than the study of the literary structure of the various books of the Bible, especially the Old Testament. Scripture warns us about people who will appear to be godly but really do not know the Lord Jesus Christ. The church has experienced what one scholar calls "the treason of the intellectual." It has been the church's liberal theologians who declared God to be dead. Theological seminaries are attacking God's Word as not trustworthy. *They are wolves in sheep's clothing.* Be warned.

- 2 Timothy 3:5: "*having a form of godliness but denying its power. Have nothing to do with such people.*"

- 2 Timothy 3:7: *always learning but never able to come to a knowledge of the truth.*"

They are always learning the Word, and can even teach from it, but deny that it is revelation from God. *The Bible is a mystery to unbiblical minds.* The technical, mechanical and scientific mind is disqualified for the recognition of the spiritual and infinite. The qualification for the perception of Biblical truth is neither philosophic nor philological knowledge, **but spiritual illumination.** One must first admit that the Bible is to be treated *as unique* in literature. Ordinary rules of critical interpretation fail to interpret it correctly.

If I want to know whether the Theologian/Author/Historian I'm reading is liberal or revisionist, I check out **what dates** they accept for certain historical events.

Will Durant, considered one of the twentieth century's greatest historians, writes "The Book of Daniel, written about 165 B.C. to encourage Israel against Antiochus Epiphanes, was circulating among the Jews who could not believe the Yahweh would let them long remain under pagan domination."[6] **Why the date of 165 B.C. and not the standard accepted date of 536-530 B.C.?** Because liberal theologians and revisionist historians cannot accept that Daniel wrote his prophecies with such amazing precision and detail because each prophecy was fulfilled exactly as predicted. Therefore the assumption by liberal theologians is that it must have been written after the fact. How could Will Durant not know when Alexander conquered the Jews? The Pharisees showed Alexander the Old Testament Scrolls containing the Book of Daniel. In Daniel's prophecies it was clearly stated what God's role was for Alexander as well as the number of nations he would conquer. Upon hearing this, Alexander would have the Old Testament translated into the Greek language (Septuagint) about **285 B.C.** and distributed through his empire. Another piece of overlooked history was the fact that the Old Testament was sealed by Ezra about **400 B.C.**

Another date that liberal theologians made up is that of the birth of Christ being 6-7 B.C. Christ died the Spring of 30 A.D. The 70th Week prophecy tells us that Christ would start His ministry at the end of the 69th week. This means that Christ started His ministry in the fall of 27 A.D. which is the end of the 69 weeks and when Jesus turned 30 years old: Both are important. The 70th week is seven years. In the middle of the 70th week Christ would be crucified, making His ministry three and a half years. This means Christ's birth would have to be September, 3

---

[6] The Story of Civilization, Caesar And Christ, Will Durant, Pg. 540

B.C. Liberal theologians and revisionist historians reject that there was a special star guiding those to Christ's place of birth. However, 6-7 B.C. has a potential natural explanation for a star event so that liberal theologians chose a date based on their bias. A "special" star is easy to believe once you know the God of the Bible.

## To the Reformed and Non-Reformed

Having been a member of both reformed and non-reformed churches I know for a fact that both are full of believers who have dedicated their lives to the service of the Lord Jesus Christ. In each church, I have been absolutely blessed with brothers and sisters who are closer to me than some of my own family. Here is what I know about both. They basically have the same essential beliefs. Both start with:

- 1 Timothy 3:16-17: "All Scripture is God-breathed and is useful for teaching, rebuking, correcting and training in righteousness, so that the servant of God may be thoroughly equipped for every good work."

Both believe in one God existing in three persons: Father, Son and Holy Spirit. Both believe that Jesus was born and was crucified on the cross as payment for our sins. Both believe in the virgin birth. Both believe Jesus is 100% human and is the Son of Man. Both believe Jesus is 100% God and is the Son of God. Both believe in the resurrection. Both believe in the Sovereignty of God, which means man's will is subject to God's will. Both believe the Holy Spirit is the one who convicts and draws us to the Savior. Both believe that ***salvation is by faith in Christ***. Both believe that once Christ is accepted as savior, the Holy Spirit regenerates the believer. Both believe the Holy Spirit dwells in the believer and begins the sanctification process to help us become Christ-like. Both believe the same about evangelism and witnessing. Both believe all are sinners. Both believe in predestination, election, the Bride of Christ and the elect. I could go on and on!

The difference is around one simple thing: Does God respect the free will that He chose to give us? God has given man free will, man only gets to choose to bend his will and knee to God. He is a beggar. Acceptance of the gift of salvation freely given **does not constitute a work**, because Scripture tells us that salvation is a gift lest any man should boast in Ephesians 2:9-10. The non-reformed believe that God's election of the elect was **corporate.** He chose to have a Bride of Christ made up of the elect. Man must use his God-given free will to choose whom He will serve.

If God selected the elect individually before time, thus overriding their free will, then *salvation is by election.* However, if one observes the reformed church's *actions you will see they believe in salvation by faith.* Their actions, like preaching, missionary spending, etc., speak louder than their theological doctrines. They are my brothers and sisters in Christ, I assure all who can hear!

If one truly believes salvation by election then why preach, evangelize or even go to church? None of that matters if I was elected before time and have a guaranteed place in heaven.

I have a good friend who has his PhD in psychology. I asked him what is going on here? He said Cognitive Dissonance. I asked what is that? *"Cognitive dissonance is the mental stress (discomfort) experienced by a person who simultaneously holds two or more contradictory beliefs, ideas, or values.* Reformed church members have to deal with the discomfort of trying intellectually to justify salvation __by election__ versus one of the clearest of all teachings in the Bible: __salvation by faith in Christ.__ I know many who go to the reformed church and are confused by salvation by election. They struggle with how a good God can create, then damn, people to an eternity in hell, and still be the loving God that the Bible states He is. **Salvation by election is a relic** left over from the War between the Holy Roman Catholic Church and the Protestants from hundreds of years ago.

R. C. Sproul, a reformed scholar/author, writes "That too much can be read into implications is obvious. This is so easy to do that even the most careful scholars can fall into it. One of the most precise confessional statements ever written is the Westminster Confession of Faith. The care and caution displayed by the Westminster divines in the drafting of the document was extraordinary. Yet in the original document there is a glaring example of drawing too much from implication."[7] We all, both reformed and non-reformed, need to know that any of us can become

---

[7] Knowing God, R.C. Sproul, 1977, Pg. 76

*editors* of the bible. As a member of a reformed church, I know there are many - like me - who do not believe in salvation by election at the individual level. Corporate, yes. They believe *in salvation by faith,* and their actions prove that they are Christians committed to being Christ's ambassadors to a dying world.

## To Our Roman Catholics Brothers and Sisters

First, thank you for your stand on abortion and similar important moral stands. If I could have one wish granted, it would be for a Vatican III. Vatican II was an amazing move of the Holy Spirit. The Catholics got their mass and sacraments to be in their own language. Reading the Bible was allowed. However, there is still much change needed. The Holy Roman Church is still a church that has many in bondage to perform works for salvation. I will usually ask a Roman Catholic, once I have befriended him/her a question: *"Do you think you are going to be in heaven?"* I ask this to get an understanding of whether he/she believes in works or faith in Christ (grace). The majority answer, *"I hope so, it depends if I have done more good than bad deeds."* What needs to happen is Vatican III, and another move of the Holy Spirit. Priests need to first get salvation by faith in Christ like the Scriptures say: Catholics need the priests to preach the Word with the power of the Holy Spirit. Also, end confessions to priests, who are mere men. We all have direct access to God and the Holy Spirit takes our prayers to God after He corrects them (read Romans 8:26-27).

## To the Jews

A Jew who believes only the Old Testament is one who has not compared the Old Testament with how Christ fulfilled the prophecies of the Messiah's first coming. Many Jews have done this comparison and have Jesus as their long awaited Messiah.

## *What can we do as Believers to help bring people to Jesus?*

- Revelation 12:11: "They triumphed over him [Satan] by the blood of the Lamb and *by the word of their testimony*; they did not love their lives so much as to shrink from death."

Do not underestimate the power of your testimony. Each person is told to be able and ready to share. We have been chosen to fit uniquely into the Body of Christ to perform our unique tasks for Him. It is as simple as sharing the story of who you were before Christ, why you put your faith in Him and what changed in your life since you chose a relationship with Christ. Yes, you have one because we all have one. I know when I hear someone sharing about God working in his or her life, it never ceases to grab and hold my attention. It always reminds me that our God is involved in our daily lives, and details are important to Him.

## Chapter 10

# CONCLUSION

I started this book with a question: ***"What brings peace, joy, happiness and hope?"***

Why do we have out-of-control crime, rampant drug addiction, widespread alcoholism, exploding STD's, rising Aids infections, a nation that is grossly obese, confusion over gender and sexual roles and lack of commitment in relationships of every kind. It is because we all have been infected with the "Sin" virus. The Bible warns us that there will be a time when good and bad are reversed. People will disregard sound teaching and prefer to be told what they want to hear. There is a solution for the ills of any nation:

- 2 Chronicles 7:14: "If my people, who are called by my name, will humble themselves and pray and seek my face and turn from their wicked ways, then I will hear from heaven, and I will forgive their sin and will heal their land."

Your life matters. We all have a theology, a belief system whether we know it or not. The decisions and actions we take are determined by what we believe. The world teaches that we have no ultimate purpose; that life is an aimless and meaningless journey which ends in death. The problem with this is that God put knowledge of Him in us. We all somehow know that death does not end life. Life is a journey from the now to eternity. It is planned by God for our good. ***The world provides us the means of life,*** *but not the meaning of life.* Suffering and death are a part of human life. Without them, there is no reason for man to seek help from God.

The life I now live is what I call *"Father Filtered."* This simply means that nothing that comes into my life is a surprise to my Heavenly Father. In fact, it can only enter my life with Him knowing it, and then using it for my ultimate good. I have been asked if I could go back and change my first twenty-two years, would I? Especially since I shared I thought God did a pretty crappy job! Once you understand that God chose that path because, in His divine wisdom, He saw that **PERHAPS** I would seek Him. It is not a question of whether your home life or family is dysfunctional, *it is how dysfunctional?* God knew that each problem/challenge/victory that was/is part of our lives has purpose. When life goes sideways, and at some point it always does, I can choose to trust Him even though I, almost all of the time, do not know why. He chose me, a person of low position, who was in need of His gift of salvation, a broken man who needed a God to save, heal, transform and rebuild him. *Because God can see the potential, He can look beyond the apparent.*

- Luke 7:41-43: "Two people owed money to a certain moneylender. One owed him *five hundred* denarii, and the other *fifty*. Neither of them had the money to pay him back, so he forgave the debts of both. Now which of them will *love him more*?" Simon replied, "I suppose the one who had the bigger debt forgiven." "You have judged correctly, Jesus said.'"

*All that I am, and all that I will have and be, is found in Christ!*

- Matthew 5:20: "For I tell you that unless *your righteousness surpasses that of the Pharisees and the teachers of the law*, you will certainly not enter the kingdom of heaven."

Jesus states that our righteousness will be higher than the Pharisees and the teachers of the law. How is that possible? When we accepted Christ, His righteousness was imputed to us. Is Christ's righteousness higher than the Pharisees? Of course it is. Here is the best part. The righteousness of all believers is equal because it is the same for each believer. *The low position of my past does not matter anymore, thanks to Christ.* I am free from the eternal grip of Satan and the concerns of this world.

- John 8:32: "Then you will know the truth, and the truth will set you free."

Knowing the Real Truth will set us free. Truth provides freedom from fear. I know that my future is secure and in God's control. I know that even in death my future is bright because of Christ. This world no longer holds sway over any believer.

- John 16:33: "These things I have spoken to you, that *in Me you may have peace.* In the world you will have tribulation; but be of good cheer, I have overcome the world."

- John 14:27: "Peace I leave with you, *My peace I give to you*; not as the world gives do I give to you. Let not your heart be troubled, neither let it be afraid."

- 2 Thessalonians 3:16: "Now may the *Lord of peace himself give you peace* at all times and in every way. The Lord be with all of you."

Peace is found in Christ. He gives it to us. Christ has overcome the world. He alone is the victor over even death. In Christ there is *rest* for all is secure in Him!

- John 15:11: "I have told you this so that *my joy may be in you* and that your joy may be complete."

Joy is found in Christ. Again he gives us His joy!

- Romans 5:2: "…through whom we have gained access by faith into this grace in which we now stand. And *we boast in the hope* of the glory of God."

Hope is found in Christ. We have His promises that we will be with Him in heaven.

- Psalm 144:15: "Happy are the people whose God is the Lord."

Happiness is knowing your God is the Lord of this universe.

***What brings peace, joy, happiness and hope?***

***They are the result of a relationship with Jesus. He gives them as gifts to us for our blessing!***

What was predestined from the beginning of time? That our good God had a plan of Great Redemption for His children. All are offered salvation by Faith in Christ.

- 1 John 5:13-21: "I write these things to you who believe in the name of the Son of God so that you may **know that you have eternal life.**"

A.W. Tozer reminds us "Throughout the Bible when the man of God set his heart to exalt God above all, God accepted his intention as fact and acted accordingly. Not perfection, but holy intention made the difference."[8]

- Deuteronomy 29:29: "The secret things belong to the Lord our God, but the things revealed belong to us and to our children forever, **that we may follow all the words of this law.**"

I am not concerned about what I cannot yet understand in the Bible, I am concerned about what I do understand, for that is what God will judge me by.

- Philippians 4:4-7: "Rejoice in the Lord always. I will say it again: Rejoice! Let your gentleness be evident to all. **The Lord is near.** Do not be anxious about anything, but in every situation, by prayer and petition, with thanksgiving, present your requests to God.

---

[8] The Pursuit of God, A.W. Tozer, 1948, p70

*And the peace of God, which transcends all understanding, will guard your hearts and your minds in Christ Jesus."*

- Romans 15:13: "May the God of hope fill you with **all joy and peace** as you trust in Him, so that you may overflow with hope by the power of the Holy Spirit."

You too can have peace, joy, happiness and hope. Trust in Christ and seek to know the "I AM" of the Bible. You can go it alone, or be under the care of a loving Father whom you can call **"Daddy."**

# Appendix

# YOUR GOD GIVEN FREE WILL CHOICE "PERHAPS"

According to God's revelation, the Bible, each of us are accountable to God. As I shared earlier, I was completely unaware of this simple fact. Even though I was raised as an atheist in a secular environment, I knew there was a God. I also had a moral barometer inside me that was given to me by God. There is an important distinction between belief and truth. Truth is not relative, but belief is. Some people think truth changes. However, it never does. What changes are our beliefs. Some people in the past believed that the earth was flat, or that the earth was the center of our solar system. Their belief did not change truth. If a proposition is true, it remains true whether or not I choose to believe it. If a proposition is false, all the belief in the world cannot make it true. Why? Beliefs are unable to change objective reality, although they do change a person's subjective reality.

The Bible has "Revealed Truth" given to man by God in a Book. That Book contains what no other book in this world has – the Seal of God, because of two reasons: **Revealed Knowledge** and **Prediction of Future Events**. In essence, revealed truth and facts that *only an omniscient God could know.*

## Example of Revealed Knowledge - Astronomical Truth Prior to Science

- Jeremiah 33:22: "I will make the descendants of David my servant and the Levites who minister before me *as countless as the stars in the sky* and as measureless as the sand on the seashore."

**Number of Stars**: *The Bible states the stars cannot be numbered.* We now know this is true. The maximum number the naked eye can see is around 3,000 to 4,000 stars. The Ancient Greeks mapped 985 stars. Science now estimates a million billion billion stars in the known universe, but believes this to be conservative.

## Example of Prediction of Future Event – 30 Pieces paid for Christ by His enemies

In the Old Testament book of Zechariah, written in 520 B.C., we find this prediction.

- Zechariah11:12: "I told them, if you think it best, give me my pay; but if not, keep it. *So they paid me thirty pieces of silver.*"

The New Testament and history confirm that Jesus Christ was sold for thirty pieces of silver. How did the enemies of Christ know to pay that exact amount of silver? They did not, and that is the point.

- Matthew 26:15: "Then one of the Twelve, the one called Judas Iscariot, went to the chief priests and asked, 'What are you willing to give me if I deliver him over to you?' *So they counted out for him thirty pieces of silver.*"

What makes this incredible is that the Jewish Chief Priests and Elders picked the value and it matches exactly what the prophet predicted hundreds of years prior. There is no way that they, the enemies of Christ, would be in collusion with regard to fulfilling this prophecy related to Jesus.

**Predictions**: Jesus Christ fulfilled over one hundred prophecies that covered his birth, ministry, crucifixion and resurrection. In college, having had to sit through classes on statistics, including the theory and laws of mathematical probability, I was taught about the probability of events occurring randomly. **_Taking forty-eight major prophecies concerning Jesus' first coming, it has been calculated that the odds of these prophecies being fulfilled in one person are one in $10^{157}$_**[9][1] These kinds of odds are so astronomical that these prophets who predicted specific events in detail hundreds of years in the future **_obviously were not the source of inspiration._**

**_The question is why do you believe you will be in heaven?_**

Given all the possible choices, there are really only seven from which to choose:

**_Salvation by Faith in Christ:_** This is what is revealed by the Bible as the only way to receive God's forgiveness and a place in heaven by His grace.

**_Salvation by Law:_** The Bible clearly tells us that the law can condemn only. Why? Because no one can keep it. When we attempt to keep the law, we will either fail and give up or become a hypocrite. Jesus called the Pharisees hypocrites because he knew they were depending on the wrong premise for salvation.

- Galatians: 2:16: "Know that a person is **_not justified by the works of the law_**, but by faith in Jesus Christ. So we, too, have put our faith in Christ Jesus that we may be justified by faith in Christ and not by the works of the law, because by the works of the law no one will be justified."

**_Salvation by Tradition (human philosophy, creeds, standards, codes or rules):_** The Bible clearly tells us the traditions, or writings, of any organization are just that: "human rules" that cannot bring salvation to those who puts their faith in them.

- Matthew 15:3-9: "'Jesus replied, "And why do you break the command of God for the sake of your tradition? For God said, 'Honor your father and mother' and 'Anyone who curses their

---

[9][1] A Ready Defense, Josh McDowell IBSN 0-89840-281-6, 1990 P.210.

father or mother is to be put to death.' But you say that if anyone declares that what might have been used to help their father or mother is 'devoted to God,' they are not to 'honor their father or mother' with it. Thus you nullify the word of God for the sake of your tradition. You hypocrites! Isaiah was right when he prophesied about you: 'These people honor me with their lips, but their hearts are far from me. They worship me in vain; *their teachings are merely human rules.*'"

**_Salvation by Works:_** This salvation is about doing more good deeds than bad deeds. The problem is: do I ever really know where I stand? When this method is chosen, you never know your fate with certainty.

- Ephesians 2:8-9: "For it is by grace you have been saved, through faith—and this is not from yourselves, it is the gift of God, not by works, so that no one can boast."

Works are important, but not for your salvation. That is by faith and is a gift of God. The book of James clearly teaches that our works do not make us righteous before God. Real saving faith is demonstrated by good works. Works are not the cause of salvation; *works are the evidence of salvation*. Faith in Christ always results in good works. Works are an outpouring of our love and thankfulness to God and Christ for such a great salvation.

- James 2:17: "In the same way, faith by itself, if it is not accompanied by action, is dead."

- James 2:26: "As the body without the spirit is dead, so faith without deeds is dead."

**_Salvation by Church:_** This teaches that membership matters. Can belonging to an earthly church or organization guarantee one's acceptance by God? This thinking benefits only one entity: the church or the organization. One is subject to the whims and rules of the group! *No religious membership can save you.* God's offer of salvation is by faith in God's provision: Jesus Christ.

**_Salvation by Election:_** This salvation is about being the special selected ones. Some teach God selected you individually and personally from before time. How does one really know? Others believe they are part of the 144,000 that will be there in heaven, although Scripture teaches there is a multitude that no one can count. The downsides to thinking you are elected is complacency and error to recognizes who God is according to His self-revelation in Scripture. God is good, just and will not violate His own character (Who He is) when it comes to the God-given free will of man. To believe that, no matter what I do, I am guaranteed I will be saved and in heaven because I was chosen by personal election by God before time. ***There is no clearer teaching in the Bible than salvation by faith in Christ.*** The Bible clearly tells us that the Jews' special election will not save them all. Why? Because many depended on election and not faith in Christ.

- Romans 9:27: "Isaiah cries out concerning Israel: 'Though the number of the Israelites be like the sand by the sea, ***only the remnant will be saved.***'"

**_Salvation by Love:_** This is the belief that God is love and all His children will be in heaven. Although this is a popular thought, it is not supported by God's Word.

One may believe only one salvation method from above or any combination of these salvation methods listed. ***Only two persons know your salvation status: you and the God of the Bible, your Creator. God's word states that Salvation is only by faith in Christ.*** This salvation will bring a personal relationship with Christ and God. ***His gifts of relationship are peace, joy, happiness and hope.***

Other Books by the Author:

**Truth – Not Exactly**
**The Final Trumpet**

Acknowledgements

*Editors: Christie M., Vicki T., Susan M., Sue C., Jennie T., Stephanie M., Bret M., Paul M., and Gianna M.*

Printed in the United States
By Bookmasters